Also by James Goodman

Stories of Scottsboro

BLACKOUT

For Steve —
    There is not much baseball
in here, but still I thought
that the New Yorker
in you and maybe even
the English teacher
might enjoy this.
    All my best wishes
            Jim

James Goodman

North Point Press

A division of Farrar, Straus and Giroux

New York

North Point Press
A division of Farrar, Straus and Giroux
19 Union Square West, New York 10003

Copyright © 2003 by James Goodman
All rights reserved
Distributed in Canada by Douglas & McIntyre Ltd.
Printed in the United States of America
First edition, 2003

Library of Congress Cataloging-in-Publication Data
Goodman, James E.
    Blackout / James Goodman.— 1st ed.
        p. cm.
    ISBN 0-86547-658-6 (hardcover : alk. paper)
    1. Electric power failures—New York (State)—New York.
2. Electric power failures—New York (State)—New York
—Psychological aspects. 3. Electric power failures—Social aspects
—Case studies. 4. Electric power failures—Psychological
aspects—Case studies.   I. Title.

HV551.4.N7G66 2004
974.7'1043—dc22

                                            2003017840

Designed by Jonathan D. Lippincott
Title page art by Susan Mitchell
Map designed by Joe LeMonnier

www.fsgbooks.com

1   2   3   4   5   6   7   8   9   10

For Jackson, Jennifer, and Samuel

It is not upon you alone the dark patches fall
                   —Walt Whitman, "Crossing Brooklyn Ferry"

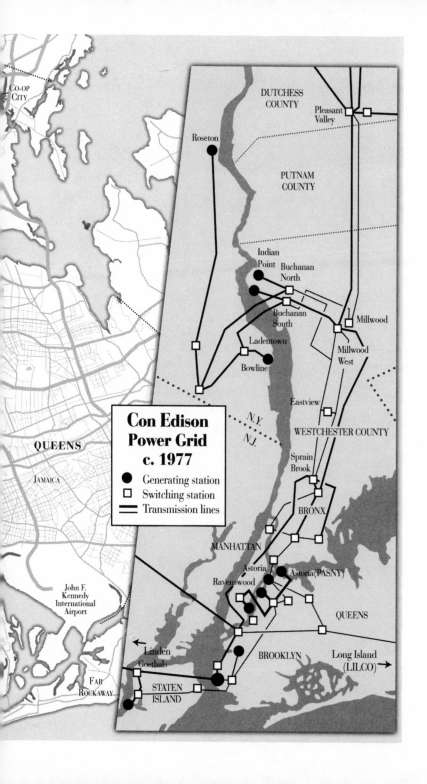

CO-OP
CITY

DUTCHESS
COUNTY

Pleasant
Valley

Roseton

PUTNAM
COUNTY

Indian
Point   Buchanan
         North

Buchanan
South   Millwood

Ladentown   Millwood
                       West
Bowline

Eastview

N.Y.
N.J.   WESTCHESTER COUNTY

QUEENS   Sprain
                       Brook
JAMAICA

Con Edison
Power Grid
c. 1977

● Generating station
□ Switching station
— Transmission lines

BRONX

MANHATTAN
                  Astoria
          Astoria (PASNY)
Ravenswood

John F.
Kennedy
International
Airport   QUEENS

Linden   Long Island
Goethals BROOKLYN   (LILCO) →

FAR
ROCKAWAY   STATEN
           ISLAND

Preface

On Wednesday, July 13, 1977, there was a blackout in New York City. It was the second big blackout in a dozen years, and those who were around for the first thought back to the crisp, moonlit evening in November 1965 when thirty million people, spread out over eighty thousand square miles of the Northeast, suddenly found themselves in the dark. The 1977 blackout was limited to the five boroughs and some northern suburbs, a few hundred square miles inhabited by 25 percent of those thirty million people. That night there was no moon, and an oppressive mass of hot air had just drifted into the metropolitan area. Meteorologists said the heat was there to stay.

In 1977, as in 1965, there was excitement, adventure, and fright in skyscrapers and subway tunnels; busy intersections and bus terminals; nightclubs, theaters, and concert halls; high-rise stairwells and department stores; elevators, emergency rooms, and ICUs. There was revelry in bars and restaurants, music and dancing in the streets. People displayed tremendous reserves of kindness, generosity, patience, and good humor. On just about every block in a city of thousands of blocks, some man or woman, boy or girl, proved himself or herself a hero. Strangers not only talked to strangers, they did whatever they could do to help them through the night.

For people who have never been in a big city during a blackout, it is a difficult night to imagine. So much of what makes New York the city that it is—the height of its buildings, the density of its population, the hours (twenty-four) of its operation, the mass of its mass-transit system, the brilliance of Broadway, the role of its business and finance in the work of the world—is made possible by electric power and light. New York City could not be New York, "The City," without them. Yet it is worth the effort to try to imagine, for on those rare nights without electricity, in a city utterly dependent on it, there is simply so much to see. All the more in 1977, when some of what people saw was more complicated and less comforting than what they had seen twelve years before.

I begin my story in the last hour of light; take in the night and day of the blackout; and then dwell in its aftermath, when people argued about why people did what they did when the lights went out. For weeks that argument raged. Countless people had their say. Yet the argument was like the night: lots of heat, little light, and despite many penetrating observations and perfectly reasonable conclusions, it ended right where it began, as a shouting match between people who held fast to one explanation and people who held fast to another.

What was missing was not intelligence or analytical sophistication but common sense, and perhaps also a desire to find common ground. Few people were willing to consider the simple possibility that there were elements of truth in several explanations, let alone some combination of explanations. Or the possibility that no single explanation, no matter how useful for explaining the behavior of this person or that, could explain the behavior of thousands of people of different ages in different places at different times.

I do not offer a grand theory or synthesis. I have not fashioned a compromise that will satisfy both sides. My way of thinking about what happened is my story about what happened, and it will not be nearly as useful as the way that most people thought about what happened at the time. When it comes to utility—observations and conclusions that suggest particular courses of action—the parsimonious have it all over the complex.

Yet we are complicated creatures, and not just when the power fails. I juxtapose the wide range of blackout behavior and the narrow range of the argument about that behavior to encourage readers (as they read, watch the news, practice politics, talk with their students, teach their children, argue the world with colleagues, neighbors, strangers, and friends) to look warily upon answers that are incompatible with every other answer, explanations (whether of apparent heroism or cowardice, altruism or selfishness, success or failure) that can be expressed in thirty seconds or less.

I tell my story in bursts, re-creating incidents, deeds, accidents, encounters, conversations, exchanges, and arguments, trying to evoke mood and place and time. I cut from scene to scene rapidly, wishing I could be everywhere at once, see every sight, hear every word, miss nothing.

As I struggled with the form of this book, I naturally imagined others. One was more traditional, a book with fewer characters and scenes, each developed in great detail and depth. Instead of juxtaposing bits and pieces of experience, I would meld them into a single story, or at least connect and clarify them with arguments, summaries, and conclusions. But I decided that a more traditional form would detract from my effort to convey a sense of the wide variety of things people did in a night and a day, and the wide variety of reasons they did them. Rather than contribute to generalizations, I hope, at least momentarily, to confound them.

There is, of course, a vital place for generalization and for social and cultural synecdoche, stories in which individuals (or a small part of a community) represent the whole. There are vast expanses of our experience, past and present, that we couldn't fully understand without them.

Yet there is something to be said for the dizzying accumulation of detail, the highlighting of differences often lost in generalizations based on the categories of census returns, public-opinion polls, and shallow social and cultural analysis. Something to be said for constructive humility as we try to answer essential but elusive questions about what moves us.

"I am large, I contain multitudes," Walt Whitman writes. And who among us does not contain, if not multitudes, at least a few? Which makes a city, let alone a city of seven and a half million, a disorderly place. This book is an attempt to give that disorder, the multitudes within us, and among us, its due.

BLACKOUT

1

Afterward everyone wanted to know why.

There had to be a reason.

People wanted to know what it was.

Or they thought they knew what it was, and they wanted to say.

Either way, they talked about it, talked in English, Spanish, Russian, and Korean; in Japanese, French, and German; in Italian, Arabic, Hebrew, and Chinese.

For weeks it seemed as if they talked about nothing else.

They talked about why, when the lights went out, people did the things that they did.

People also wanted to know why the lights went out in the first place.

Not everyone, but some:

Reporters. Mayor. Governor. City, state, and federal regulators. Certain customers. Even the president of the United States, who happened to have a keen interest in energy.

So they talked about it, and they asked Con Edison officials, who also wanted to know but would have preferred not to talk about it. They asked Con Edison to explain what went wrong.

There had to be a reason.

People wanted to know what it was.

Con Edison officials said it was lightning.

They hoped it was lightning.

Lightning is easy to explain, and there is no one, on earth, to blame.

Or they thought they knew what it was, and they wanted to say.
They thought there was a reason, one reason.
One reason for all the things those people did in the dark.
One reason for the things they do.

Electrical engineers said it was more complicated than that. Lightning may have played a role, but to say that lightning caused the blackout would be like saying the wind caused the capsizing of a poorly designed sailboat sailed by an inexperienced or even incompetent captain and crew.

Almost everyone agreed there was a reason.

There was lightning.
Not so much in the city, but just to the north, in the rocky rolling hills of Westchester County, the precious wedge of New York State that sits atop the Bronx. So much lightning that in Oradell, New Jersey, a budding scientist, nineteen years old, who climbed out on his roof after hearing severe storm warnings on the radio, could see it, great bolts in deep dark clouds. He stood thirty miles from the storm.

But people disagreed about what that reason was.

Half the city's power came through Westchester.
It traveled along conductors, thick transmission cables, each made up of many strands of wire hung on hundred-foot steel towers. The towers were laid out like a letter Y—albeit a Y drawn by a very young child. The top of the Y leaned so far to the left (which was west) that its right fork pointed due north.

The right fork brought power from upstate New York and New England. The left fork brought it from three power plants along the Hudson River: Roseton, an oil-burning plant in New-burgh; Bowline, another oil-burning plant, twenty-six miles to the south; and Indian Point, a nuclear power plant on the other side (the east side) of the river. Left and right forks met in Mill-wood, like busy lanes of southbound traffic, and merged into a congested corridor of towers, power lines, and substations in the west-central Westchester towns of Pleasantville, Eastview, Sprain Brook, and Dunwoodie. South of Sprain Brook and Dun-woodie, the lines went underground.

So they argued: raised their voices, shook their heads, waved their arms, pointed fingers, as if they were hammering invisible nails.

And argued.

It is not anyone's idea of a perfect system. If Con Edison had had more land at its disposal, it would have run its transmission lines over soil that was less rocky and therefore less resistant to electricity; it would have built more towers and put fewer cir-cuits on each one. But Westchester is squeezed between the Hud-son River, the southwest corner of Connecticut, and Long Island Sound. Land is expensive, wide-open space scarce. Rights-of-way are hard to come by.

They had strong feelings and opinions.

The stakes were high.

Lightning struck right in the middle of that corridor, at 8:37 in the evening, in the midst of a ferocious storm. It struck a tower carrying conductors between substations in Buchanan and Millwood, 345-kilovolt lines that supplied 1,200 megawatts of power from Roseton, Bowline, and Indian Point.

The arguments took some nasty turns.

It was New York.

It was July. It was 1977.

Many people were in sour moods to begin with.

2

In the city, around the time of that first bolt of lightning, knowing nothing of the storm in Westchester or the shape of the power grid or the responsibilities of a system operator or even the source of all the electricity—6,000 megawatts—they consumed on a summer night, people did the things that city people do.

Some talked.
Some walked.
Some waited for buses.
Many worked: in hot kitchens and hotter subway stations; in cool, quiet offices after hours; in fire stations and precinct houses; in factories and warehouses; in bridge and tunnel tollbooths; in hospitals, machine shops, hotels, and stores of all kinds.
Some hailed cabs. Some drove them.
Firemen fought fires; policemen fought all kinds of crime.

There were a few signs but no warnings, and except for a few operators and dispatchers at a few power plants, substations, and control centers, no one knew anything was wrong.

At around nine o'clock, the time of the second lightning strike, people watching television might have noticed the picture on their sets contract.

Not many of them thought anything of it.

Not even those who knew, as one Queens man knew, that a

shrinking picture was a sign of either a failing TV tube or low voltage.

The Queens man had much more faith in his television than in Con Edison, and though critics of Con Edison were more common than hot-dog carts in midtown, few of them knew as much about electricity as he did. He was an electrical engineer, and from 1958 to 1964, the chief engineer of the city's Bureau of Gas and Electricity.

People ate, on the late side: burgers and french fries; bagels, ribs, and baklava; pizza, plantains, and pork-fried rice; falafels, hot dogs, and shish kebabs; soggy soft pretzels and shaved ice; sausage bread on Arthur Avenue; striped bass in Astoria; dainty portions of veal and duck; oversize turkey-and-chopped-liver clubs.

The electrical engineer expected bad service and lame excuses from Con Edison, and he was rarely disappointed. In August 1959 a blackout had shut down the West Side from Columbus Circle to Columbia University, and a large part of the Upper East Side. Asked by the mayor to investigate, he found that the design of Con Edison's grid was at fault: too few feeders from too few substations, increasing the likelihood that small problems would lead to large ones. He conducted similar investigations after the mid-Manhattan blackout of 1961 and the Brooklyn blackout of 1962.

Con Edison always blamed someone else, or something else.

The electrical engineer always blamed Con Ed.

Some drank their dinners, in a mostly futile effort to beat the heat: frozen daiquiris, tequila sunrises, White Russians, Black Russians, banshees, and margaritas; frosty mugs of beer chasing shots of whiskey; seven-ounce bottles called ponies; twenty-five-cent quarts.

Some uncorked fine wine; others twisted the tin tops off Boone's Farm, Night Train, and Mad Dog 20/20.

When the lights went out in November 1965, the electrical engineer was in a tunnel beneath the East River on a Manhattan-bound D train. The train rolled to a stop. Four hours later, when the train's battery-powered emergency lights began to dim, he grabbed a trainman's lantern, climbed out of the rear of the train, and walked back to the Brooklyn station. His fellow passengers spent another nine hours underground.

Some sat on rocks or rooftops in the heights of the outer boroughs, marveling at the Manhattan skyline. Others hurried out of the city's big parks before dark, kicking soccer balls, bouncing basketballs, swinging golf clubs, tossing Frisbees and softballs, twirling bats like batons.

People sang in the shower. People played music in the street.

Some people prepared for bed. Others were already sleeping. Some people were married. Others decided to separate or get divorced. Thousands of people were out of work. Some of them pored over the classifieds; others found that work, for wages, was not the only way to get by.

The 1965 blackout began when a surge of power, well within normal operating range, tripped an improperly set relay at the Beck power plant in Queenston, Ontario. The tripped relay opened the circuit on one of five lines carrying 1.5 million kilowatts of electricity north and west into Canada. The other four circuits overloaded, and the power from Beck reversed itself, sending a massive jolt of electricity south into New York. The surge overwhelmed protective devices. One feeder failed, then another. Within ten minutes, New England Power and Con Edison knocked themselves out trying to fill upstate New York's void.

Some listened to the game: the Yankees were in Milwaukee.

At Shea Stadium, twenty-two thousand watched the Mets.

Young men and women, in from Westchester, Long Island, and New Jersey, shopped for secondhand jeans, records, rolling papers, and marijuana. Many danced: to funk, to country, to punk, to Israeli music at the 92nd Street Y, and most of all, to disco.

People looked for prostitutes; prostitutes looked for johns.

Some watched *Baretta*; others said, "I've seen this one," before checking to see if anything else was on.

A relay in Canada, Con Edison said, caused the blackout.

Not quite, the electrical engineer replied. The relay certainly contributed to the blackout, but a precipitating event is not the same as a cause. A week after the blackout, he briefed reporters on the highlights of his twenty-two-page report. Con Edison, not Canada, was responsible for Con Edison's troubles. The utility needed to learn how to free itself from neighboring utilities when they threatened its stability, and it needed to install automatic load-shedding equipment, which would help its engineers manage the available load once New York, or some significant part of it, was on its own.

People stepped off trains: at Grand Central, at 125th Street, at Fordham Road in the Bronx.

People snatched purses.

People stepped onto trains, as a Long Island couple did at Penn Station, a few minutes after nine. They'd tried to take the 5:04, but when they learned that it would be delayed by a tunnel fire, they opted for dinner at the Steel Palace and tennis: Billie Jean King and Virginia Wade, playing for the New York Apples. As the 9:20 to Manhasset pulled out, at 9:20, the Long Islanders congratulated themselves on their city savvy.

And people had their purses snatched.

———

At around nine o'clock, the picture on his television set contracted.

The electrical engineer didn't think anything of it. Brownouts (tactical voltage reductions, intended to protect the system at times of extra-heavy usage) and mini-blackouts had become as much a part of summer in the city as smog. His lights often flickered and dimmed. It had been a 90-degree day, and it was a sultry night. There had been scattered electrical storms. Every air conditioner in the city was running on high.

The lights flickered. He didn't even get up from his chair.

Two dozen people stood in line outside a reasonably priced Italian restaurant.

A famous critic had recently raved about the food.

In newspaper offices and television and radio studios, people gathered the latest news.

The president defended his opposition to federal funding for health clinics that performed abortions even if it meant that only well-to-do women would have the right to choose.

Life, he said, isn't always fair.

Residents of Rockwood, Tennessee, returned to their homes a day after an overturned truck released a cloud of bromide gas. National guardsmen patrolled to prevent looting. Government officials said that one-third of the trucks on the highways were unsafe; without more inspectors and stiffer penalties, there would be horrible disasters.

At around nine-thirty, subway motormen began to report trouble with the signals, the red, amber, and green lights that help ensure a safe distance between trains.

Some were flickering.

Others were out.

There was no pattern to the outages, nor obvious meaning.

The supervisor on duty at the Transit Authority's subway command center had heard nothing from Con Edison.

People went to mass; people went to minyan.

People played mahjong; people played bingo.

Sharpies played three-card monte with two or three shills, each of whom won hand after hand.

Tourists saw fistfuls of twenties, and on the cardboard-box card table they thought they saw the red queen the sharpies seemed to work so hard to hide. They put down twenties of their own, and lost them every single time.

Some complained about the heat; others said, "Why complain, you can't change it."

People played bridge, and people took bribes.

The subway supervisor, who had worked for the Transit Authority for twenty-nine years, had been on duty for his share of difficult nights and days, including the rush hour in November 1965 when the lights went out with half a million people underground.

He had also seen his share of changes, particularly since 1965.

The trains were ancient, covered with graffiti, and horribly maintained. Stations were menacing: dilapidated, filthy, dark, and dreary. Panhandlers were everywhere. Ridership was way down.

But at the moment, with the signals on the blink, the city's curse was a supervisor's blessing. There were only forty-five thousand people on 175 trains along 714 miles of track.

A few people hid from Son of Sam.

Many people worried about him, including two sixteen-year-olds who, spooked by their own speculation about the serial killer at an eerie moment just before dark, decided to return to their Co-op City apartments. They had to pass through a long walkway in the center of a shopping plaza; after sunset, it was like a tunnel without lights.

"He's in there!" one of them cried.

"But we're not with boys," the other said.

"And we're not in a car."

"And who comes to Co-op City, anyway?"

They took no chances. They pulled their bell-bottoms up to high-water level; drew their sweatshirt hoods around their heads until only their noses showed; locked arms; and walked with their stomachs sticking out as far as their stomachs would go.

Lots of people smoked pot; people with lots of money snorted coke.

"I could see it coming," said the supervisor, "from the first reports of temporary loss of power." There were too many for it to be a coincidence.

He did something he'd never done—something no one, as far as he knew, had ever done in seventy-three years of subway service. He asked dispatchers to ask the motormen on all 175 trains to proceed to the nearest station and stop there.

People opened fire hydrants.

People swam in pools.

People worked for wages despite welfare rules.

Children ran under sprinklers; others played war with water guns to keep cool.

Parents kissed kids good night; people who hardly knew each other screwed. Women waited in line for ladies' rooms; men walked right in and pissed.

The Transit Authority supervisor may have wondered why Con Edison had not warned him. But he had no reason to feel left out of the loop.

The police knew nothing. The fire department knew nothing. The mayor knew nothing.

The chairman of Con Edison himself knew nothing.

He had just finished dinner, at home in Bronxville. His workday was over. Despite the heat and the staggering demand, the system was humming along. He was on his way into the den.

Some shot heroin. Some shot hoops.

Some ran from the police.

Some studied: for summer school, for the real-estate-licensing exam, for the LSATs.

Some stiffed waiters; some left huge tips.

Some burned abandoned buildings for landlord's cash.

Some burned them for kicks.

The chairman had come to Con Edison from LBJ's Department of the Interior in the shakeup after November 1965. The design of the system and much of the equipment, he immediately discovered, were outdated. Service was spotty. Management was cumbersome, with too much weight at the top. Con Edison was a company customers loved to hate.

The chairman promised reliability, efficiency, conservation, and clean air. He lowered the retirement age to sixty-five and, breaking with company tradition, replaced retirees with executives from the outside. He saw to it that transmission lines were strengthened, plants modernized, control centers equipped with the latest load-shedding equipment, and emergency procedures streamlined. He worked especially hard to turn public opinion around, pulling the DIG WE MUST signs off excavation sites and opening an office devoted entirely to fielding customer complaints.

People planned weddings, people planned christenings.

People planned holdups, hits, bar mitzvahs.

Some read the ticker in Times Square: North Korea had downed an unarmed U.S. cargo copter, killing three.

Others read novels, billboards, air-conditioner-installation manuals, playbills, train schedules, maps, menus, concert programs, and poetry.

Politicians gave speeches.

People listening wanted to know what they proposed to do about crime.

Sidewalk preachers said Judgment Day was coming; wherever you looked, there were signs.

Despite the chairman's best efforts, the early 1970s were difficult years. Eighty percent of the company's generating capacity came from oil at a time when cartel and embargo contributed to price hikes as high as 400 percent. Clean-air regulations prohibited the company from switching to cheap crude, let alone coal. Energy consumption was rising, but steady inflation, cost overruns, and environmental concerns stalled the construction of new generating plants. The company's stock sank, and in 1974, for the first time in ninety-one years, Con Edison skipped its quarterly dividend.

The chairman sold two plants to the state and won approval for steep rate increases. By 1977 he had begun to turn things around. Revenues were up. Profits were up. The stock was on its way back up and once again paying a quarterly dividend.

Some jumped subway turnstiles or entered though broken exit gates; others decided to walk or take a cab; beneath city streets, nine o'clock was late.

People argued about welfare. People argued about the Middle East: Begin's ministers had approved a plan, but Sadat said that without justice for the Palestinians and a return of the occupied territories, there would be no peace.

————

Con Edison's customers were as unhappy as ever. They'd invested heavily in the company's revival ($700 million since 1975, in higher monthly gas and electric bills) without hope of interest or dividends. New Yorkers now paid over 10 cents per kilowatt-hour, twice what they had paid in 1972.

You couldn't please everyone. Overall, things were going well. Very well. On July 10, the chairman had been a guest on ABC's Sunday morning television talk show. "I can guarantee," he said, "that the chances of a brownout or a blackout are less than they have been in the last fifteen years, and that the chances are less here than in most other cities in the United States."

People woke for work, dressed, and grabbed a bite to eat.

Others returned, juggling briefcases, Chinese takeout, six-packs, and apartment keys.

Some got drunk.

Some got high.

A few teenagers in from the suburbs looked half-sick when two cops walked by. The cops shook their heads; one even smiled. They're cool, a kid said. They have bigger fish to fry.

Those kids were a complete mystery to the cops. Not because of the 1960s hair, the beads, beards, or bandanas. Certainly not because of the marijuana. But because they could have been under a canopy of leafy trees. On a screened porch. In an air-conditioned room. By a backyard pool. At a place at the beach. Yet they chose to spend the evening on a stinking-hot city street.

The chairman walked into his den and turned on the hi-fi, which was tuned to WNCN, a classical-music station. He picked up a magazine and sat down in his chair.

The reception was terrible. He called to his son, all ready to "bawl him out." He assumed that the young man had been "fiddling" with the receiver.

———

Some stepped into elevators.

Others stepped out.

Strangers passed strangers.

Some said hi.

Others nodded, shrugged, wondered, sighed.

Some laughed. Some cried.

People were born. People died.

People asked questions: Who, how, what, when, where, and why?

3

In sealed buildings, the first thing people heard was a deep, labored thunk, the dying breath of everything electric, all at once.

What was that?

"We aren't moving."

"Push it again."

One of the passengers pushed it again. Nothing happened. And again.

"Try to open the doors."

The large car was crowded. A passenger pried open the doors, and the passengers spilled back into the restaurant, greatly relieved.

"The elevator's out," one of them said to the bell captain, pointing toward it with the impatience of an important person who has had a bit too much red wine to drink and red meat to eat.

The bell captain pointed, too, toward the window, the restaurant's main attraction, 107 floors above the street.

Moments before, the view had been a drunken expressionist's floor-to-ceiling canvas, a riot of electric light. Now all you could see was a line drawing so simple and sober on a canvas so big and black that at first glance you couldn't even see it. Long white lines lay like moonlight on a large body of water: the headlights of cars driving into the city from Westchester and Long Island. Red lines of taillights showed the way out. Down in the harbor, out in the Upper Bay, up along the Hudson, the red, white, and green navigation lights of small boats, which on any other night might have been lost in the haze, suddenly looked bright. And the torch of the Statue of Liberty (which got its power from New Jersey) looked like a white fire in the sky. Across the river, in Hoboken and Jersey City, it was just another summer night.

"The elevator's out."

"So's New York," the bell captain said.

On a low floor of a high-rise in the middle of Harlem, a seventeen-year-old sitting by an open window heard a great roar—like the roar at the stadium, after a Yankee hits a game-winning home run; or the Garden, after an audience realizes, a few bars into it, that the band has begun to play a favorite song. Then she heard a cacophony of sighs, laughs, shrieks, cries, whistles, hoots, gasps, howls, curses, groans, and screams.

She thought the world was about to end.

She grabbed her fourteen-month-old son and her sister's babies.

Her mother turned on a transistor radio.

The anchorman was excited, but not alarmed. It was a blackout, not a bomb.

"Where's New York?" asked a pilot as he prepared to land a cargo plane, carrying crates of strawberries, at Kennedy Airport.

One second the city was there. The next it was gone.

The flight controllers had no idea.

"Proceed to Philadelphia," one of them said.

"What am I supposed to do with the berries?" the pilot asked.

"Eat them," the controller answered.

Subways slowed, stopped, sat, lurched forward, crept, stopped again. Lights flickered; some cars went completely dark. Air-conditioning shut down, if it had been running to begin with.

Conductors said nothing. Passengers on the trains that made it to a station—all but seven—or that crawled in on emergency power just after the system went down had no way of knowing, or reason to believe, that anything extraordinary was wrong. Especially if the station had a few emergency lights.

Some, fed up, walked out and up to the street.

But many stayed put, intending to wait out the delay. It's just another night, one man said, on the MTA.

Simon Hench, the lead character in *Otherwise Engaged*, was alone onstage when the lights went out and the music, a record playing on a turntable, skidded to a stop.

Had it been just the music, the audience might have thought it was part of the play. Hench's only desire was to sit, alone, and listen to his brand-new recording of Wagner's *Parsifal*. But every time he put stylus to vinyl, he was interrupted: first by his tenant, who had woman and money troubles; then by his brother, who had job troubles; then by a friend, who was having an affair with his (remarried) ex-wife; then by the girlfriend of the friend, who came by (braless, and before long blouseless) in search of a publisher for her book; then by an old prep-school mate, now the frustrated suitor of a young woman Hench had slept with on the sofa in his office a few days before; then again his brother, who informed Hench that Hench's wife was having an affair; and finally Hench's wife.

"What do we do now?" he asked.

"There was mass confusion," said a twenty-one-year-old who, at seventeen, had given up high school and hopes for a college football scholarship for the service. Now, four months out of the marines, and work, he was shooting hoops in Brownsville.

His friends hooted and hollered, dashed this way and that. A moment or two passed before someone realized it wasn't just in the projects that the lights were out.

"What have I done?" asked people who had just blown out birthday candles, shut heavy windows and doors, struck street-light and utility poles with bats and sticks, slammed down telephone receivers, flicked switches.

"What did you do?" others asked them.

"What now?"

Others knew.

For them the question was not what or why but who, and when, and how.

Mayor Beame had been speaking about mortgages to a standing-room-only crowd in a Co-op City synagogue when, in the words of a reporter, the lights "flickered, dimmed, and died."

As aides and synagogue staff tried to figure out what had happened, the mayor kidded his audience about the importance of paying bills on time.

He had many enemies. But even allies acknowledged that the lights had dimmed on his administration two years earlier, when investors (suddenly purporting to be "shocked!" at the sleights of hand by which the city balanced its books) stopped bidding on its bonds. With the city on the brink of bankruptcy, the mayor's fiscal powers passed to two state agencies, the Municipal Assistance Corporation and the Emergency Financial Control Board. As those agencies pressed the city to freeze hiring and salaries, cut spending, and dramatically reduce services, the boss became a broker, a go-between among labor unions, state and federal officials, fiscal overseers, bankers, and other powerful money men.

By July 1977 the worst was over.

But the city, like the nation, was still mired in troubles, material and spiritual, and many people had concluded that the seventy-one-year-old Democrat was not up to the job. He had six challengers for his own party's nomination, and the primary was two months away.

All kidding aside, the mayor assured his audience that despite the recent wave of foreclosures at the fifteen-thousand-unit middle-class housing project in the Baychester section of the Bronx, neither the city nor Con Ed had turned off their lights.

A Brooklyn couple, on their way home from the movies, had just stepped onto a Bushwick-bound bus.

The ride was slow, but steady.

On the walk between bus stop and home, he decided to go back out.

Why? she asked. She didn't understand.

She pleaded with him.

They argued.

But his heart was set.

"How will I ever identify Mr. .44 now?" a Bronx woman wailed.

He was Son of Sam, the .44-caliber killer. She fit the profile of his victims perfectly: eighteen, long brown hair, hanging out on the steps of her friend Theresa's house, across the street from Westchester Square Hospital, with her boyfriend, Tony. Police had warned young couples to stay off the streets, and especially out of parked cars. At least they weren't in a car.

She'd seen him again, she had just told her friends, who were tired of hearing it, seen him on the subway ride home from her class at the Eastern School for Physicians' Aides. "I knew it was him," she said. "I was positive. I've seen enough composites to be able to pick him out of a crowd."

Now she could not see a thing.

"What did you do?" a young woman asked her boyfriend.

It was a rhetorical question.

The television had died, and she assumed he hadn't paid the electric bill.

He went to the window. For a few moments, people stood still, as if stunned or frozen by the great patches of darkness that had fallen on them. Slowly at first, then faster, they began to move, en masse, toward Broadway.

The Cubs' Ray Burris was in mid-windup.

The Mets' Lenny Randall, at the plate.

The arc lights above the field and seats went off, along with the lights in the corridors, concession stands, and ramps.

Burris held on to the ball.

Randall thought the game was over: "God. I'm gone. I thought for sure He was calling me. I thought it was my last at-bat."

Con Edison's acting vice president for public affairs had just returned home, "horribly hot" and bothered, from a class at Columbia, where she was working, virtually full-time, toward an MBA.

Home was a sublet on West Sixty-sixth Street, around the corner from the utility's Energy Control Center. She'd taken the place a week before, shortly after leaving her husband.

Wanting nothing more than a shower and some sleep, she turned on the radio, took off her clothes, and turned on the water. She was about to step in when the newscaster began to slur his words and the lights went out.

"Oh shit," she said.

She managed to find her way to the phone and dial the number of Con Edison's Central Information Group. "CIG," a colleague answered.

"This is Joyce. I'm here in Manhattan. The lights just went out. What's going on?"

"We lost the system," he said. "Lightning."

"I'm two blocks away," she said. "I'll run over as soon I get dressed. Tell security if any media show up, keep them down on the sidewalk until I get there."

She had hung up the phone and started to get dressed when it occurred to her that if she hadn't known what was going on until she called, perhaps the chairman didn't know. She went back to the phone.

"Chuck, it's me, Joyce, in New York."

"Joyce," he said. "I am sitting here in the dark, in my den, in Bronxville. Bronxville's dark. And I can't get through to the Westchester control room to find out what's happening here in Bronxville."

"Forget about Bronxville," she said. "Forget about Westchester. I just got off the phone with CIG, and we lost Manhattan. We lost the whole system."

4

In a city of seven and a half million, plenty of people kept doing what they had been doing, or tried to, or went on to do what they would have done on any other night.

Up in Windows on the World, people lit candles, mixed drinks, cooked and served food, bused tables, drank, smoked, ate, even sang.

In the lounge, a jazz trio played.

Men slipped off sport coats and suit jackets—the dress code was a dead letter—and removed already loosened ties.

Security stood by the exits, hoping to discourage those who disliked the heat or the smoke—or simply the thought that they were stuck 1,250 feet in the air—from taking the stairs.

One man had been reading a newspaper under a streetlight at the intersection of Seventh Avenue and Christopher Street called Sheridan Square.

When he lost that light, he took a few steps to his right, until he was next to the emergency light at the top of the subway stairs, and there, despite the horns, brakes, sirens, and screams, he continued to read.

For people looking for cabs, all that had changed were the odds.

Some of the fortunate few who found one paid dearly.

Not every cabbie could resist the temptation to abandon the

Taxi & Limousine Commission's rigid regulations for the elastic laws of supply and demand.

An apartment full of people on West Tenth Street had been celebrating, in candlelit rooms, the union of two men.

The power went out.

No one noticed until one of the hosts tried to turn on a fan.

All three television networks transmitted from New York; it was Wednesday, prime time.

NBC and CBS had backup power, and ABC switched its transmission and programming to Los Angeles so seamlessly that *Baretta* was back on the air before the detective solved the crime.

Police rode into Washington Square Park on horseback and asked the people partying in the waterless fountain to leave.

One group ran to Bleecker Street and back, snatching candles from café tables.

By the time they returned, the police were gone.

The fountain was again full of people, getting high or higher on angel dust, LSD, Thai sticks, Hawaiian, and hash.

One dealer, moved by the apocalyptic magic of the moment, gave away his stash.

Stoop hangers sat and stood on stoops.

People watchers watched people.

Dog walkers walked their dogs.

Whistlers whistled.

On East Sixty-first Street, a man on a stoop whistled at a woman walking her dog. "Hey, beautiful," he said.

She said, "How can you tell?"

"It's a citywide blackout," Simon Hench told his audience after huddling with stage managers, who had lugged out several lanterns and set them up as footlights. "You have a choice: Leave the theater now, get tickets for another night or a refund. Or sit tight for the half hour left in the play."

The audience voted for the play. Hench picked up right where he left off. When it came time for the next teasing aria of *Parsifal*, he hummed it. The audience rose and cheered wildly, then rose again at the end.

A young man in an East Side restaurant gently tapped his date's hand.

She had just finished her dessert.

Lights on, lights off. He led, but she knew the steps.

They stood up and left.

Two Jersey women, both divorcées, learned about it from the attendant at the Lincoln Tunnel tollbooth.

They'd met at a party a few weeks earlier. One, only recently divorced, had complained that after twenty-five years of marriage, she didn't have a clue how to meet men. "Singles bars," the other said. "I'll show you."

The recently divorced woman wanted to turn back.

Her new friend would not think of it, and it was her car.

They continued on in.

The young Bronx woman who had been with her boyfriend on the steps of her girlfriend's house was sure it was "him."

She tripped on the curb. Stumbled into a trash can. Smacked people with her outstretched arms. A car backfired. Maybe it was a gun. She started to run, past Ruthie's, past Sid's grocery, past Pigeon's. Right into a mailbox.

Back home, she was calmed by her sister's hysteria.

It wasn't *him*, her sister said. It was me. I turned on my hair dryer, curling iron, and fan all at once and blew some big fuse.

———

Four men, each carrying a golf club, had been on their way up Amsterdam Avenue.

They began to poke out store windows.

One window after another, almost nonchalantly, as if they simply liked the sound.

At Bellevue, the city's busiest hospital, gas generators installed in 1966 kicked right in, allowing doctors and nurses to continue to make their rounds.

Network television was back on the air, but who had a battery-powered set?

"It's radio's night," one reporter said.

The leading stations all had backup power or transmitters in New Jersey.

WNEW and WABC went all-news; WCBS and WINS were all-news already.

WMCA stuck with the Yankees.

Fans who turned on transistors didn't miss a pitch.

"There was fear mixed with excitement," said a Brooklyn man who had been driving along Eastern Parkway.

People stood around in groups, wondering what was going to happen.

The man worked for a moving company. He tracked down two friends, and together they hurried to the lot where he parked his thirty-eight-foot van.

Sound sleepers, in bed early, slept right through it.

Others decided that bed was the place to be.

One was that seventeen-year-old in Harlem.

The world hadn't ended. It had been a long day. Despite the heat and the noise from the street, she was soon sleeping as soundly as her fourteen-month-old son.

In a pub on Seventh Avenue in Brooklyn, two dozen police officers from the 78th Precinct and numerous friends of the force, all of whom had come from the softball field where they'd been since the end of the 8-4, dashed out the door.

The owner put candles on the bar.

People began to sing.

"Fantastic," a man out on the street yelled, "fantastic! It's the whole city! It's the whole goddamned world!"

The owner locked the door.

One patron said, "It's going to be a beautiful night."

People who stole for a living stole more.

On Reid Avenue, in the Bedford-Stuyvesant section of Brooklyn, several men removed the lock on a liquor-store gate with a heavy-duty lock cutter, drew guns, and went in. A few stood watch, waving others away until their partners had taken what they wanted, including the cash register.

There were dancers who kept dancing, singers who kept singing. Where they could make themselves heard without electricity, bands played on. At *Beatlemania*, at the Winter Garden, the faux John, Paul, and George put down their electric guitars, picked up acoustics, and led the audience in a singalong. Ringo didn't miss a beat.

Standing by the window of his East Village apartment, the director of an anti-poverty organization heard gunfire and watched small groups of kids grow. He rushed out, as he so often did, to try to talk those kids (half of whom were out of work, money, and patience) out of trouble.

On Utica Avenue, a group of men ripped the gates off of Muslim Jewelry, owned by a Crown Heights community leader.

Eleven minutes into the blackout, they'd cleaned out his store.

The men of Ladder Company 26 delivered a gas generator to Mount Sinai Hospital and then sped to a fire in an abandoned West Harlem school. Ordinarily, they would have tried to save the building. But with so many calls so suddenly, they didn't have the numbers, equipment, or time. Instead they surrounded it, poured water in, and waited for it to collapse.

To the delight of the audience at the Vivian Beaumont Theatre, the cast of *The Cherry Orchard* raided the supply room for the company's alternate production, *Agamemnon*, grabbed a handful of candles, lit them, and finished the second and third acts of the Chekhov play.

A truck pulled up in front of a Warren Street gun shop, a block from City Hall. A few men climbed out, removed the gate, forced open the door, loaded their truck, climbed back in, and drove off.

Many writers kept writing.

One was a nineteen-year-old who just *had* to write about her day at Coney Island with her cousins, who were visiting from Puerto Rico; about her younger brother, who (without a summer job) was hanging out with hoodlums and headed for trouble; about the sound of Donna Summer singing the theme song from *The Deep* as the lights dimmed, then brightened, then died; about the "hair-raising roar" from the street and the staccato slap of rubber soles on pavement as the boys bolted from the housing-project plaza to Columbus, Amsterdam, and Broadway.

She lit candles and set two of them right above her diary, but she still had to duck down so low her nose almost touched the page.

She heard a hiss, then smelled something "foul," a home perm burning.

She patted out the fire and ducked back down to the page.

On Fulton Street, near Nostrand Avenue in Bedford-Stuyvesant, one gang stole furniture while another stole bicycles. A jeweler who was still inside his store called the police, and they came quickly, but most of the furniture and eighty bikes were already gone.

In the lobby of the Waldorf-Astoria, hotel staff greeted guests with candles and champagne glasses and urged them to relax—and stay put—until Con Edison turned the lights back on.

On Broadway, four blocks south of Columbia University, a man backed his car up onto the sidewalk. Three men stepped out. One attached one end of a chain to the car's bumper. Another attached the other end to the accordion gate protecting a Tech Hifi. When the third said, "Go," the driver stepped on the gas, tearing the gate from its hinges and anchor bolts.

One man tossed a metal litter basket through the window.

All four went to work emptying the store.

Three men pulled three cars up onto the sidewalk in front of the Mansion Coffee Shop, on York Avenue. They pulled right up to the window, left their engines running and their headlights on.

The owner and cook, standing in the window, smiled.

The men, cabbies on break, went back in and finished their sandwiches, coffee, and pie.

On Brooklyn's Broadway, not far from Decatur, people huddled in small groups, heads darting this way and that.

One man hopped into a car and drove it into a sports shop. A crowd followed, knocking the owner to the floor.

The owner fled.

The last looter set the empty store on fire.

At Fifth Avenue and Fifty-sixth Street, their corner six nights a week and Sunday afternoons for two years, the Linden Woodwind Quintet would have liked to keep playing, and for a few minutes they tried.

But they needed to see their music, and even with members of the audience holding up matches and lighters, they couldn't see well enough to play.

They apologized, divided up the gate, packed up, and walked away.

A man in his late teens or early twenties punched out the window of Al-Bert's, a Bushwick men's shop, and loaded the inventory into a stolen van.

He used a chain, the van, and (instead of his bleeding hand) a garbage can to open up an appliance store farther up Broadway.

He stopped to help an older man put a sofa on top of a station wagon.

Back home, he unloaded televisions.

"Plug them in," his mother urged. "See if they work."

The stage manager of *The Merry Widow* had two flashlights. He aimed one at the soprano, who was in the middle of "Vilia," then handed the other to the conductor. The cast used lanterns as footlights and a cast member's motorcycle headlight as a spot.

Ladder Company 26 left the abandoned school on the West Side for a furniture store on the East.

They crossed on 116th Street.

At Lenox Avenue, "blacks," all armed, guarded a mosque.

At Pleasant Avenue, "Italians," all armed, had formed a cordon with a row of cars to ensure that the looting on Third Avenue didn't spread to their block.

Firemen rushed into the burning building.

Looters carting sofas and chairs rushed out.

"No thank you," said a woman at the Waldorf to the waiter pouring champagne. What she wanted was to know how much longer the wait would be.

She went from concierge to concierge.

None of them knew.

She decided to take the stairs.

A gang of twelve surrounded a token booth at the Halsey Street subway station and told the clerk, who had barricaded the door, that if he didn't hand over his tokens, they'd kill him. He handed over nearly five thousand, worth 50 cents apiece.

Reporters rushed out to the streets, up to the Control Center, over to the hospital, down to City Hall.

Their editors edited.

Editors at the *Daily News* had already put Thursday's paper to bed. But, spurred on by word that their archrival, the *New York Post*, had canceled Thursday's paper, they went to work on a new headline—BLACKOUT!—and a couple of new stories.

The publisher, meanwhile, placed phone calls to the publisher of Long Island's *Newsday*, hoping to persuade him to print it.

"High-class dudes" were out early in the evening, said the Brooklyn man with the moving van, street-smart criminals who "left the wine alone and went for the Scotch and bourbon."

He and his buddies knew just what they wanted.

Cans of salmon and tuna to sell to poor folk, baby food and Pampers.

Clothes, stereos, and color TVs for people with jobs.

They drove the van to Utica Avenue.

On the thirtieth floor of a midtown hotel, five men and two women, all employees of an association that accredited agencies serving the blind, had gathered with Dictaphones and braille typewriters to prepare a report. The men, without sight, kept working; the women couldn't, but they said nothing until the end of the meeting, at which time the men, and their dogs, escorted the women back to their rooms.

At the corner of Third Avenue and 105th Street, several men removed the steel curtain protecting one of Morris Toyland's four entrances. Once inside, they went right for the bicycles, which were in a separate room, up a flight of stairs.

Young people in from the suburbs to hear disco, jazz, or punk rock, to buy beer (without an ID) or pot, to people-watch, to talk to friendly strangers, to hang out on the streets after dark without being hassled by hard-ass cops, lit joints they would have lit sooner or later, to celebrate the darkness.

Across the street from Con Edison's corporate headquarters, which were at the intersection of Irving Place and East Fourteenth Street, several young men removed the gate and smashed the window of a music store. As they were about to enter, a man tried to stop them. They knocked him to the ground.

The woman climbing the stairs at the Waldorf lived in a suite in the tower apartments atop the hotel's twenty-seventh floor. Twelve flights up, she ran out of breath and sat down to rest.

———

Up Amsterdam from the guys with the golf clubs, there was a furniture store, Capri Furniture. A car pulled up. A man stepped out with a chain and went to work on the gate.

At the yeshiva on Eastern Parkway, students dashed around looking for candles. They found hundreds on the rabbi's table, and by the light of those candles, they prayed.

On the Queens side of the Fifty-ninth Street Bridge, a small group of teenagers opened a bank of pay phones with baseball bats and filled their pockets with change.

In Central Park's Delacorte Theater, Jenny was singing "Pirate Jenny" in *The Threepenny Opera*.
The orchestra stopped.
Jenny kept singing.

"All the lights are out, everywhere," someone said, on that basketball court in Brownsville. Nobody knew what to do.
Until someone said, "Let's get Pitkin Avenue."

Here and there, muggers mugged.

Everywhere (in hotels, apartments, and houses; in bathtubs and showers; on beds, floors, and couches; along dirt paths and on patches of grass; on sandy beaches and wooden benches; in no-longer-air-conditioned clubs and littered alleys; on the hoods of cars and in horse-drawn carriages; deep down in waterless fountains and in elevators stuck in office towers), blissfully oblivious sweat-soaked lovers made love.

5

The argument about the causes of the blackout began when Con Edison's acting vice president for public affairs, unable to satisfy reporters with science and technology, turned, in desperation, to theology.

She was out in front of the Control Center, where she'd been since shortly after she hung up the phone, finished dressing in the dark, and made her way down twenty-nine flights of stairs. It was only when she stepped outside that she realized she didn't have her glasses on. She had taken them off for the shower. She could hardly see without them, but the Control Center was just down the block. No way was she going back up those stairs.

She arrived at the same time as the first reporters.

The chairman arrived fifteen minutes later and went right inside.

Con Edison's president was already inside, working with the system operator.

The chairman was called to the phone. It was the mayor, who wanted to know what had happened, why it happened, why he hadn't been warned, when the power would be restored.

The reporters also wanted to know why. There had to be a reason.

The president talked about lightning.

The chairman talked about lightning.

The acting vice president talked about lightning. She explained that an impossibly improbable succession of lightning strikes—four, five, maybe six, unforeseen and unforeseeable—

had tripped protective relays and circuit breakers, opening conductors all over Westchester, vital links to the north.

She expected full restoration in a few hours.

"Lightning?" a reporter asked incredulously. "This is a modern system. This is the twentieth century. How could lightning cause this? Lightning strikes everywhere. All the time. Aren't redundancies built into the system?"

She glanced across West End Avenue, where there was an empty lot, and beyond it nothing but the highway and the Hudson River. Even without her glasses, she could see that in New Jersey the lights burned bright. She wished the Control Center were located in the middle of the island.

She repeated what she had said about relays and breakers, about the tremendous imbalance between supply and demand.

Reporters persisted, asking the same question—why?—every which way.

Finally, she threw up her hands. "Look," she said. "It was lightning. It was an act of God."

6

Some people kept doing what they had been doing, or tried to. Others did things they had never done before.

The Bushwick teenager whose girlfriend had thought first of the electric bill ran out the apartment door and down four flights of stairs.

"Come on, man," he said to his young cousin, playing at the bottom. "It's a riot."

His cousin jumped back. "That's when they come in and shoot you," he said.

"No. That's when you take what you want from the stores."

On Broadway, four men had rocked a parking meter off its base and used it to break down the door of a jewelry store.

The men went in. Others followed. Some had baseball bats, and when they went to work on the display cases, small bits of glass took flight.

The younger boy took a piece in the cheek.

The older took two watch cases off the floor.

Outside, a cop pounded the sidewalk with his nightstick. Three other cops stood by.

The boys sprinted for a block, then stopped.

"Shit, man," the older boy said.

The cases were empty.

"All that for nothing. I was scared in there. My heart was doing a heavy tango."

———

Passengers on the seven subways stuck between stations braved a city space ordinarily occupied only by maintenance men, delinquent juveniles, graffiti artists, and rats. Led by motormen and transit police, they stepped from cars to catwalks, clutched railings, inched their way toward emergency exits and up steep emergency stairs.

It was frightening for everyone.

The air alone (a fetid stew of cooked cables, brake pads, brake linings, urine, and sweat) overwhelmed a few.

But a business-school student was certain he was not the only one who enjoyed it, as he might have some harrowing mountain adventure. An urban Outward Bound.

"Everyone's living out his fantasies," said a woman standing in the middle of a midtown street, waving her arms to and fro.

A few minutes earlier, she had been in a subway, stuck between stations.

Now she was directing traffic, like a pro.

"This is the night," she said, "that everyone who wants to be a traffic cop can be one."

"We are all black now," said a man on Manhattan's Broadway.

Two others picked up a trash can and used it to ram and loosen a variety store's iron gate.

A crowd gathered.

A police car pulled up, and five officers stepped out. The crowd backed off.

The officers squeezed back into the car and drove off.

One man broke the window.

Many went into the store.

"Hey, I want to do that," said a young woman as she and a friend drove up Madison Avenue in his Volkswagen Beetle. He pulled over at Sixty-fifth Street.

Directing traffic was easy.

The trouble was her white barebacked sundress.

When headlights hit it, drivers and pedestrians could see right through it.

She and her friend got back in the car and continued up the East Side.

"Somebody's got to do the job," said the man in the intersection of Eighth Street and Seventh Avenue in Brooklyn. He was an employee of the Harlem Development Corporation.

"The cops and firemen don't live here anymore. So we got to do it ourselves."

"It won't be long now," a concierge told one guest after another—there were hundreds now—in the Waldorf lobby. Until then, he said, handing out candles and champagne flutes, "the wine is on the house."

The guys with the golf clubs kept walking. But the glass they shattered sounded like a starter's gun: Hundreds of people dashed from apartments to streets and from streets to stores.

The volunteers in the intersections were not the only ones living out fantasies. In the alley behind Badlands and the Ramrod, the two bars at the corner of Christopher Street and West Street, clusters of men—some with their shirts off, others their pants down, all emboldened by the thought that no one who wouldn't like what they saw was going to be able to see, danced, kissed, groped, gave, and received.

"There was no need for preliminaries," one man said. It was welcome relief from "the usual tedium," the "uptight, ritualized procedure, bar-hopping and man-hunting."

———

Police informed the mayor that the lights were out all over the city. He found his way back to the podium and shared the news, quickly reminding his audience that he was working to reduce off-hour express bus fares to Manhattan, close a nearby landfill, and shut down a porn shop that had opened in their shopping plaza.

Back at Gracie Mansion, he huddled with campaign aides, who had been meeting there. When he emerged, he briefed reporters in the driveway: He had just declared a state of emergency. He was on his way to City Hall.

The men who opened Capri Furniture went in first, but a huge crowd followed. Those more interested in footwear than furniture left for the fully stocked shoe store across Amsterdam Avenue.

The more experienced of the two New Jersey women led the way into the candlelit room, walked up to the bar, and planted herself between two men.

The newly divorced woman froze.

A few minutes later, her friend rose and walked toward the door, arm in arm with one of the men. "We'll be back," she said.

The other man approached the newly divorced woman.

"When is the last time you were laid?" he asked.

She spun around and darted out the door.

Although they had never done it in the dark, the four hundred cleaning women who worked nights at the World Trade Center knew, from fire drills, just what to do. They left their vacuum cleaners and carts and followed the emergency exit lights to the stairs.

"I'll be back," said Boz Scaggs, promising a rain date.

He knew his songs by heart but needed electricity to play.

His audience of nearly three thousand quietly made its way out of Avery Fisher Hall.

A few men had broken through one of Morris Toyland's doors. A crowd broke through three more and smashed every pane of glass on both the Third Avenue and 105th Street sides of the store.

A woman who lived near the Long Island Rail Road tracks in Woodside, Queens, packed picnic baskets with sandwiches and drinks and, together with her children and neighbors, carried them up the embankment, where passengers on the 9:20 to Manhasset had been stranded, in cars with very few windows that opened, since 9:36.

Residents of a Brighton Beach senior citizens' home carried candles, flashlights, water, and (in some cases) medicine to the doors leading to the emergency stairs on their floors. There they waited for several dozen of their neighbors, who had been out on the boardwalk and were climbing, in a human chain, to their rooms.

Most of them had never set foot in the stairway, which, like most high-rise stairways, was menacing in the brightest light.

The building was eighteen stories.

They were all in their seventies, eighties, and nineties.

Several of the climbers lived at the top.

The Brooklyn man whose wife had pleaded with him to stay home hopped on his bicycle and rode straight to a bicycle store on Flatbush Avenue.

The owner stood in the door.

The man rode to another. The owner was out front, with a big dog.

————

Two women and a man on their way up Eighth Avenue spotted a young woman outside the Port Authority Bus Terminal, looking lost and frightened.

She knew she wasn't going to get a cab. She didn't know whether it was safe to walk uptown.

"We'll make it safe," said one of the women walking up Eighth. "Nothing else to do. All the customers be scared to go into hotel rooms with no lights."

"Oh, there's been some trouble," said the woman walking with her. "I seen six kids jump one guy before, and it made me sick. But most of the night people, we don't want that. We want to go about our business. Because this is America."

The cast members of *Oh! Calcutta!* were caught without their clothes on, and the doors to the dressing rooms, up a narrow flight of stairs, were locked.

"When the lights go on," one cast member called out, "we want the audience naked and the cast clothed."

The Newbergers, an elderly couple from Illinois, stepped forward with his seersucker jacket and her raincoat, and others followed their lead.

Those forced to walk through tunnels and up and down stairs often got their names in the papers, but most New Yorkers did their walking, some of it rather remarkable, on sidewalks and streets.

Five and a half miles from Manhattanville to Mount Eden, crossing the Harlem River on the McCombs Dam Bridge, Yankee Stadium a great black bowl on the Bronx side.

Eight miles (nearly a mile of which was the Verrazano Bridge, high above the Narrows separating the upper and lower New York Bay) from Brooklyn's Ditmas Park to Staten Island's Dongan Hills.

Nine miles from Shea Stadium, in Flushing Meadows, to the

Port Authority Bus Terminal, just in time for the one o'clock bus, the last bus back to New Jersey.

Ten miles from a concert in Central Park to apartments near Prospect Park.

Eleven miles from jobs in Greenpoint to homes in Bergen Beach.

Twelve miles, just for the hell of it, from Battery Park, at the bottom of Manhattan, to Inwood, at the top.

Seventeen miles from Coney Island, Brooklyn, to Ravenswood, Queens.

A crowd followed a brick through the window of LeMans, an Amsterdam Avenue men's shop.

As looters departed, arms full of shirts, slacks, sport jackets, suits, and socks, a middle-aged black woman flailed at them with a broomstick.

"No, don't do it," she pleaded. "Please. They worked so hard. Don't. Don't."

Residents of a welfare hotel took turns shining flashlights on the woman directing traffic on West End Avenue at Ninety-fourth Street. The woman was petite, and her neighbors, worried that cars wouldn't see her, had outfitted her in bright white poster board and bedsheets.

The owner of Morris Toyland, a captain in the police auxiliary, directed traffic near his Inwood apartment until a neighbor relieved him, freeing him to drive down to the 23rd Precinct, which was a few blocks from his store. There he baby-sat for children whose parents had been arrested, and helped sort and catalog loot: dresses from Tessies; sneakers from Tom, Dick, and Harry's; and many toys from Morris's.

———

The young Brownsville man who had left the basketball court for Pitkin Avenue was all charged up, but he had no plan. He went into a gift shop and an electronics store. Then a jewelry store. "Everyone" was coming out with "gold and diamonds and rings."

His mother was outside their apartment house when he returned. She asked him about the loot and told him not to get caught, but she didn't get on his case.

Forty minutes into the blackout, Bellevue's generator failed.

There was no one in surgery, or late in labor.

There were fifteen patients in intensive care, eight of them on respirators. Nurses, respiratory therapists, and pulmonary residents rushed to their side and began to "bag" them: squeeze air into and out of their lungs by hand.

At the Metropolitan Opera House, the National Ballet of Canada's orchestra was nearing the end of the overture to the second act of *La Fille Mal Gardée*.

The curtain was about to go up, but never did.

The orchestra played on.

A harpist did a solo of "Dancing in the Dark" as ushers led patrons out of the hall.

In the intersections of Rego Park, some volunteers had lanterns.

Others had flares.

One had a whistle. "I used to be a soccer referee," he said. "I've lived here twenty-five years. This is my chance to help the community."

A block away, employees led customers out of Alexander's with flashlights they'd grabbed off the shelves.

They could hear people searching for the people they'd been shopping with.

And they could hear people stealing.

"Should I?" "What if they go back on?" "Oh, hell, just stuff the suit in the bag."

People in need of assistance on East Forty-second Street were drawn to the lights near the corner of Second Avenue, then heartened by the sight of numerous policemen.

The lights were real; the cops were not. A film studio had borrowed the block and the facade of the great gray newspaper building rising above it. The policemen were from Metropolis, and the building had a new name.

"This is your lifetime fantasy," said an eighteen-year-old girl from Akron. "Getting stuck in front of the *Daily Planet* in the dark, waiting for Superman. Where the hell is he when we need him?"

Up in the newsroom, illuminated by lights borrowed from the set, *Daily News* editors redid their first few pages, then sent the entire paper's copy out to Long Island, where *Newsday* printers began printing it.

Two hundred people stormed the showroom of Ace Pontiac. Within an hour, they had driven fifty cars out of a single showroom door, their feat made somewhat easier by the fire law requiring the dealer to leave keys in the ignition of each car and a few dollars' worth of gas in each car's tank.

In the emergency room at Bellevue, the flow of patients was remarkable, the injuries routine: "run-of-the-mill stab victims, punch victims, blunt trauma, sticks, clubs, fists," said one doctor on a cigarette break.

The most serious injury he'd treated occurred when an elderly woman, on her way to the lobby for the mail, tumbled down a flight of stairs.

"It was X rays the old-fashioned way," said a nurse. "The doctor looked—and then he diagnosed."

The woman had fractured ribs and a collapsed lung.

Working by the light of a police lantern, the doctor placed a tube in her chest to reexpand the lung. Exactly how many ribs she had broken, he couldn't say.

The lights went out at the Broadway Theatre during the final act of *The Wiz*.

Cast members walked to the front of the stage.

"I want a refund," someone in the audience yelled.

"Let's not be rude, darling," the Wicked Witch replied. "You've seen most of the show."

Thirty minutes after he returned to the Waldorf from a postponed play, a Boston businessman started up the stairs. On the landing of the twelfth floor he encountered "a tiny elderly lady," too "exhausted to continue to her suite in the towers."

He picked her up and carried her to her room.

She thanked him, and identified herself: Mrs. Douglas MacArthur.

She was seventy-nine.

In a grocery store on East Eighty-sixth Street in Yorkville, a man spotted a woman stuffing a bag of ice into her handbag. When he threatened to call the manager, she put it back and left.

The manager said that other customers had tried to steal pineapple slices, pork and beans, even soup. When he spotted them, he quietly asked them to return the items to the shelves.

"Go figure it out," he said. The cheapest rents in Yorkville were $400 to $500 for one small room on a low floor.

The bag that woman stuffed the ice into was a Louis Vuitton.

"Why would anyone in a neighborhood this rich try to steal a can of food?"

On the commercial strip in Jackson Heights, teenagers with flashlights took charge.

At one point a young man stopped a police car.

Then he turned and drew an ambulance through.

When the power went off at *The New York Times*, editors had the first eight copies of the eighty-page first edition in their hands.

They had an offset printing press, capable of printing a forty-page paper, in Carlstadt, New Jersey.

And they had reporters in the streets.

They didn't have an offset camera in New Jersey, but they had friends at the Hackensack *Record* who did.

So they cut and pasted, eliminating forty-two pages. Then a few of them, together with a few writers and technicians, piled into a delivery truck and left for New Jersey.

In Jamaica, Queens, a small crowd stormed the VFW Hall. Once inside, their interests varied: Some carried out typewriters and adding machines; others, bottles of whiskey, wine, and beer.

"Hey, don't let those two guys out of here," shouted a quick-witted student in a Columbia University seminar for teachers of the blind. "Those two guys" were the two blind students in the class. Initially, they'd been confused by the commotion. But as soon as their classmates told them what had happened, they took over, leading their teacher and classmates out of the class-room, through the corridor, down the pitch-black stairs, and out of the building. Then they walked over to the long line of people at a line of rotary pay phones and began dialing people's calls.

The sidewalks and streets of the theater district were filled with people and cars the way that they'd be filled with water in a flood.

Some thought they heard gunfire.

There was no mistaking the sound of breaking glass.

A few people panicked.

More would have, said a New Jersey woman who had come out of *The King and I* with her six-year-old daughter, had it not been for the "kids" directing traffic in the intersections.

"All you heard about afterward was the 'black looters,' " she said. "Well, those kids were black, and they weren't looters, and there is no way we would have made it out of the city without them."

All over the city, people who had never even stiffed a lousy waiter left bars and restaurants without paying for their drinks and food.

They did it in fine steak houses; they did it in greasy spoons.

Some had sensed an unusual opportunity. Others, sitting in the dark, their food half eaten or half served, had decided that a meal on the house was their due.

Four guys in New Lots did it without thinking; they'd been in a coffeeshop with the munchies, eating cheeseburgers and fries.

Then there were the policemen who rushed from the pub in Park Slope. They thought: *This is an emergency. No time for niceties.* None of the regular rules applied.

7

The argument about the looting began in the middle of it, when merchants who had been in their stores when the lights went out, or returned to them soon after, were asked to explain it.

"Animals," said the owner of a Brownsville garage as he watched a crowd torment the owner of a candy store on Pitkin Avenue. "Oh, those scum, those bastards, those rotten scum."

"They hate everybody," said a pharmacist on Upper Broadway. "It doesn't matter if you're a middle-class white person or a middle-class black person. They love to see anybody else hurt, because it makes them as low as they are.
"And they are the lowest of the low."

"They're crazy," said the owner of an ice-cream store on Fulton Street as a swarm of youths raced by. "They're taking their shoes and breaking windows. They're animals. They should be put in jail—and throw away the key. The cops are doing the best they can. There are about five hundred of them in the street."

"In the last blackout, people were like human beings," said the manager of a furniture store. "These people are like animals."

"The looters," said a jeweler in East Harlem, are "human animals."

8

The math was simple.

There were thousands of looters in more than a thousand stores on scores of streets in a dozen neighborhoods.

And there were very few policemen.

In Bushwick, a community of ninety thousand, there were fourteen officers on duty; in all of North Brooklyn, home to more than a million people, there were 189. The numbers were at least as lopsided in northern Manhattan and the Bronx, and police in the Bronx also had to contend with a riot at the Men's House of Detention. Like the looting, the riot started moments after the lights went out.

In no neighborhood were more than a fraction of the residents looting. But in New York's neighborhoods, the turnout of even the smallest fraction could make an enormous crowd.

Most of the stores that were saved were saved by store owners themselves, with help from employees, hired guns, neighbors, and friends. On Fulton Street in Bedford-Stuyvesant, a group of Sunni Muslims dressed in purple berets, blue blouses, blue pants, and jump boots, and armed with five-foot-long oak shovel handles, kept looters from entering Restoration Plaza. Restoration was the community center and complex of offices and shops built by the Restoration Corporation, the community development corporation established by activists a decade earlier with the support of senators Robert F. Kennedy and Jacob Javits. The

Muslims were employed by Dagger, Inc., a private security firm that took its name from another of their weapons.

Unable to keep the peace, the police tried to contain the unrest.

"Turn on your sirens," a precinct supervisor in Brownsville told his officers, "and every light. Come and go quickly. Try to make it seem that there are many more of you than there actually are." Early on, it made little sense to arrest looters; each arrest took at least one officer off the street.

"Make arrests," he said, "only when . . . you can't scare them away."

Farther west on Fulton Street, the owners of Pioneer Foods, described by grateful neighbors as "five Arab brothers," defended an entire block.

"They were riding their cars up and down the sidewalk, swinging bats and waving their shotguns," said the owner of a furniture store a few doors down.

"Two, three stores, they tried to break in, and we beat them," one of the brothers said. "When they see the shotguns, they run."

Police hoped to scare the looters.

Sometimes it worked the other way.

The sergeant in charge of the 24th Precinct, on Manhattan's West Side, had fewer than twelve cars, counting his, to patrol twenty-five square blocks. A few minutes into the blackout, he spotted a large crowd removing the gate from a Broadway stereo store.

"You are destroying your own neighborhood," he said over his loudspeaker. "Go home."

The crowd responded with jeers and bottles. One man tossed a garbage can toward the car.

The sergeant called for backup, but his radio was dead.

He asked his driver to drive on.

On 172nd Street in the Bronx, just off the Grand Concourse, a grocer who had seen a crowd enter a nearby sporting-goods shop grabbed two toy guns from a rack and, with shoe polish, painted them black.

She gave her husband one, and together they stood in the front of the store.

Looters approached then quickly retreated. Soon after, her husband's brother arrived with real guns.

Some looters and lookouts stood their ground when the police arrived.

Most fled.

If the police gave chase, other looters took their place.

If, instead of chasing, the police remained in front of a store, the looters went into another.

"It was," said an officer on patrol with three others on Broadway in Brooklyn, "like chasing the wind."

On the Grand Concourse, where the crowd occupied all six lanes of roadway and two median strips, the owner of another sporting-goods store stood guard with a shotgun, backed up by several heavily armed friends. Looters entered fifty-four stores in the area. They didn't touch his.

The Brownsville looter said his first trip to Pitkin Avenue was all fun.

His second trip was business.

He was "bent on making some cash," thinking not about what he wanted but about what he could sell. He was looking for the "most expensive things" he could get his hands on before the lights came back on. He "knew it wouldn't be too long."

He had a stereo in his hands when a shot rang out, then another. The store owner, an "Israeli" or "Arab," was shooting.

"Let me get my own ass the hell out of here," the looter said to himself. On the way home, someone jumped him.

He dropped the stereo and ran.

On Manhattan's Third Avenue, between 102nd and 103rd streets, residents rallied to repel looters. Sometimes they stood alongside store owners; sometimes they stood in their place.

"We know these people," one young man said. They were like family. "How you gonna destroy somebody you know?"

When police dared to get out of their cars, they did so in groups of three or more.

They commanded looters to stop where they were, to drop stolen merchandise, and to disperse.

Sometimes they didn't bother with the first two.

"Go home," one cop told a looter with his arms full of loot. "And by the way, maybe you can do *us* a favor sometime."

Two Jerome Avenue merchants pulled their cars up onto the sidewalk, shining the headlights into their stores.

With their engines running and their interior lights on, they just sat there, making sure everyone who passed by could see their machetes.

Two officers who had just dumped their first carload of looters at the 23rd precinct house received a call for backup from a cop who was by himself on the edge of a crowd outside Morris Toyland.

The detective and his partner pulled up with their siren on, jumped out in the middle of the crowd—by then in flight—and grabbed six looters. While the detective's partner held them by the car, the detective and the officer who had called them went into the store, flashlights drawn.

They heard noise upstairs.

The detective went up.

A dozen kids charged out of the darkness.

His partner found him flat on his back at the foot of the stairs and rushed him to Metropolitan Hospital. "They ran over me like I was a doormat," the detective said.

On Utica Avenue, a man guarded his tailor shop with a gun and a German shepherd. A group of men ordered him out of the way. He threatened them with the gun and the dog.

Gunshots sounded from a nearby rooftop.

The men didn't budge.

"I got ten cans of potash upstairs," the man said. "I'm going upstairs now. If you come up the stairs after me, I'll blind you."

He went up; they left. A few doors down, a larger group followed a man through a plate-glass window.

Word spread.

"Window-shopping" on the avenue.

"The police aren't shooting or even busting heads."

"It's a joke."

Kids, and many older folk, rushed to the nearest commercial strip.

They didn't want to miss it.

The police commissioner called for reinforcements, ordering every off-duty cop—eighteen thousand officers and seven thousand supervisors—to report to the precinct closest to his home.

The trouble was that half his men lived in the suburbs of Westchester and Nassau counties, and most of the city dwellers lived in Staten Island and Queens. Few off-duty officers were needed in the precincts closest to their homes.

They had to be transferred by bus, van, or car.

Then they had to be dressed and equipped.

"I was overjoyed to hear I was getting a busload of guys from Staten Island," said a captain in Brooklyn's besieged 81st Precinct.

"But when they walked in the door, they looked like a tennis team."

On Willis Avenue in the South Bronx, a crowd entered the Sneaker King, a mini-mall of four connected sneaker stores in which every wall was lined, floor to ceiling, with sneakers. The last looter left with the last sneaker.

On Second Avenue and 109th Street in Manhattan, a fifty-year-old baker stood in front of his bakery with his dog and a .32-caliber pistol. His cases were stocked, and people passed wide-eyed.

"You come into my place," he said, "I shoot you." That was enough.

On Broadway and 146th Street, the west side of the neighborhood known as Hamilton Heights, a crowd entered a shoe store, a sewing-machine store, and a discount store, stealing, in addition to the entire stock of each store, typewriters, adding machines, cash registers, and a safe that weighed a thousand pounds.

It didn't necessarily take machetes and .32s to keep looters at bay.

Each time they approached the window of the feminist bookstore at the corner of Ninety-second and Amsterdam, across the street from the heavily looted Capri Furniture, the owners took aim with flashlights. Each time the looters turned away.

Emboldened by the sight of so many friends and neighbors in the street, and by the restraint of the police, people who did not initially loot joined in.

Unfortunately for many of those who waited, the restraint of the crowds ("They could have had us if they wanted us," one officer said, "and they didn't want us") and the arrival of reinforcements had emboldened the police.

Even if the police didn't get them, savvier looters often did. When the Brooklyn man with the moving van had taken what he wanted from the stores, he parked the van a short distance from a commercial strip and took what he wanted from other looters.

"Hey, I got a truck for all this stuff," he'd say to looters as they staggered out of stores with more merchandise than they could conceivably carry all the way home. When the truck was full and the looters were back in the store, the man and his buddies would drive away.

Not every act of resistance was successful.

Some employees were knocked down, held at gunpoint, chased from their stores.

Or simply ignored.

With looters at work on their gate, employees of Furniture and Things, on Columbus Avenue, retreated upstairs. They shone flashlights down at the first ones in, and when that didn't stop them, they poured buckets of water.

Then they watched helplessly as looters emptied their store.

Across the street from the second bicycle store, the Bushwick man gave up on the idea of a new bike. He thought about riding back home. It was getting late, and looters were everywhere, running "like a pack of wild dogs," joining together to yank down gates.

The owners of LeMans, the men's shop, had been celebrating a birthday when a friend arrived with the news that looters had broken into their store.

They got there shortly after eleven.

"You dirty sons of bitches," one of the owners screamed.

A few looters stopped to apologize, but they didn't stop stealing.

On Broadway in Manhattan's West Nineties, youths streamed out of a shop with radios and television sets. Police grabbed a young boy and girl but withdrew when bottles began to fly. The police returned with reinforcements, wielding nightsticks, and arrested a few looters and bottle throwers.

Some of the looters carried televisions and stereos into the station house with them.

On 138th Street in the Bronx, the owner of Superior Furniture, who had just arrived from his home in Flushing, flagged down a passing police car. He told the officers he didn't care about his stock. Seventy percent of his customers were working stiffs who bought on liberal credit. He wanted his books.

The driver pulled up onto the sidewalk, and two officers followed the owner into his store. But before they could leave, a crowd of several hundred people gathered outside.

They radioed for help. Two cars came quickly, and the crowd dispersed.

On East Ninth Street, near Avenue D, a boy who had just seen looters break into a small clothing store telephoned the police and then shone a flashlight at them, hoping to scare them away.

The boy knew the owner, who'd been on the block for thirty

years, and like many of the neighbors, he liked the man very much.

The police arrived and chased the looters, but as soon as the police left, the looters returned and cleaned out the store.

Not much more for a ten-year-old to do but cry.

The Bushwick man was about to ride home. But everyone was getting something for nothing. Not far from the second bicycle shop, a crowd broke into a store. The Bushwick man was with the crowd, but on the outside. He just stood there, talking.

"Things started flying out," he said.

His hands were full.

A police car pulled up and the next thing he knew, he was inside it, in cuffs.

By early morning the police had the manpower to throw their weight around.

And they did.

They made running tackles, grabbed people by the hair, and pummeled people who resisted arrest.

But with the possible exception of the tackled, grabbed, and pummeled, observers agreed that even then the police remained cool and calm.

Some of that calm was department policy.

In the 1960s, officers often infuriated rioters and protestors by wielding nightsticks indiscriminately and shooting over their heads. Since then, training in riot control had emphasized restraint.

They were permitted to charge, with nightsticks if necessary, to "break up unruly crowds of looters."

If civilians, fellow officers, or they themselves were in mortal danger, they were permitted to fire their guns.

But they were expressly prohibited from firing to protect property.

The owner of the Radio Clinic stood on the Broadway median and watched looters empty his store, which his father had opened in the 1930s. When he could bear no more, he crossed, approached a looter, and said, "Get out of here."

"Why don't you get out of here," the looter bellowed.

He did.

Some of the policemen's calm was resignation. "By the time we got enough men to do anything," said one Brooklyn captain, "it was already too late."

Looters streamed into Key Food on Broadway in Bushwick, then came out pushing shopping carts full of groceries.

By early morning there wasn't much left.

"Fuck the whole thing," said a man in the back of the store as he set the place on fire.

Some of the policemen's calm was cynicism.

If they want to destroy their neighborhoods, more than one officer said, let them.

On Myrtle Avenue in Brooklyn, there were teenagers on both sides of the night. Twenty-five advanced upon the A&P only to be repelled by the manager, his clerks, and a security guard, a seven-foot-tall Jamaican brandishing a machete. Six others, armed with baseball bats and iron pipes, roamed a three-block radius, helping numerous merchants chase looters from their stores.

Some was politics, fiscal-crisis frustration.

The police union was in the middle of a bitter contract feud with the mayor, who was struggling to cut spending.

At one point a journalist rushed over to a cop to report a Flatbush Avenue fire.

"Tell the mayor to put it out himself," the officer said.

Just one supermarket was untouched on Broadway in Bushwick.

A decade earlier, people would have explained the owner's good fortune by pointing out that he was a "brother."

This time many brothers lost their stores.

Now people explained it, just as confidently, another way: The owner stood guard with his brothers, three clubs, and a dog.

"The word on the street," said a policeman, was that "he'll do a real number on you if he catches you messing with his store."

And some of the calm was good common sense.

"If we'd have shot just one person that night," a Brooklyn cop said, "we'd have had a war on our hands."

At one a.m., there were more than a thousand people in and around the A&P on University Avenue in the Bronx.

Or a bloodbath.

Two officers stood outside a Utica Avenue A&P, watching as hundreds of people, including scores of women and children, did their grocery "shopping." Anticipating the anger of looted merchants, one of the cops answered a question merchants would repeatedly ask him by asking a question of his own:

"How," he asked, "can you shoot anybody here?"

9

Badly outnumbered, poorly equipped, and sometimes the target of looters hurling rocks and bottles and bricks, policemen were also moved to metaphor.

"It was like a fever struck them."

"The looters swept through here like locusts."

"I've seen looting before, but this was total devastation. Smashing, burning, as if they'd gone crazy. They were like bluefish in a feeding frenzy."

"You grab four or five, and a hundred take their place. They were like animals."

"In 1965 we were dealing with human beings. Now we are dealing with animals."

"It's the night of the animals."

10

So much depended upon where you were and what time you were there.

"This is the greatest," said a twenty-year-old in Rego Park. "People aren't afraid to come out of their houses. There are so many people on the street, nobody's getting mugged."

"I want to go home," a Brooklyn woman cried as she and her fiancé drove down Nostrand Avenue in Bedford-Stuyvesant.

A gang of young men had just charged down the block "like a herd of elephants, yelling, 'Blackout, blackout.' "

Until then the couple had no intention of letting one dark street spoil a romantic evening.

It took them an hour to return to her apartment, twenty blocks away.

The stadium light and sound crew started a gas generator.

The Mets chairman addressed the crowd: "This is the safest and coolest place to be."

The chairman didn't identify himself. Fans would have booed, as they had been booing mercilessly since June, when he traded the beloved Tom Seaver to Cincinnati. This was not the time to provoke them. He had already closed the concession stands.

Half a dozen players took the field and, by the headlights of two vans, pretended to play. They pitched, hit, ran the bases, even slid. Afterward they signed autographs along the railings.

The organist played "Jingle Bells" and "White Christmas." Thousands of fans sang along.

A Manhattan psychiatrist, eager to see how people would respond, left his Lexington Avenue office and walked over to Park Avenue.

It was quiet and gloomy.

Cars crawled without honking. People walked without a sense of direction. Apartment houses stood above the dark streets like tombstones.

It seemed, he said, like "the end of the man-made world."

"What's up?" a reporter asked a young man and woman walking along Queens Boulevard.

Their smiles glowed in the dark.

"Remember what everybody did the night of the big blackout," the young man said. "We're going home."

An NYU undergraduate was already home, alone in his East Fourth Street apartment, all ears: first gunfire out front of the Hells Angels headquarters; then breaking glass; and then (just as he was about to go to sleep, or to try) a scream, a woman's scream, wholly unlike the other screams, screams of surprise and glee, that had been coming from the street. It was "awful," he said, "a long bloodcurdling scream."

Up and down the "alphabet" avenues just to the east, community activists built bonfires, collected money for beer and batteries, and posted sentries outside stores whose owners treated their customers well.

Drinkers drank, smokers smoked, dancers danced to salsa, rock, and mambo.

One group of revelers, hoping to ward off troubles worse than a blackout, sacrificed a cat.

There was some looting in the East Village, but not much. Had there been none, one activist said, the blackout would have been just plain fun, like a festival or feast.

Faintly at first, the psychiatrist heard the sound of bagpipes. The piper was a professional who'd started a mile north. He had a following. The psychiatrist joined them, cheering each new song.

"There was a riot in the street," said a television producer in her thirties, who, along with her husband, an advertising executive, lived on Amsterdam Avenue.

They saw the guys with golf clubs.

They saw people pour out of the projects.

He called 911.

They saw men with sofas, bureaus, and dressers.

The line was busy.

Women with lamps, mirrors, and chairs.

He tried the local precinct.

Children with pillows and small tables.

Busy, too.

He called a precinct across town.

"Sorry," the desk sergeant said. There was nothing he could do.

"We were trapped," the woman said. "They could have burned our building down, they could have stormed the building, killed people. . . . That's what was really scary—the total absence of law and order."

On Stillwell Avenue in Bensonhurst, a three-year-old followed her parents onto the front porch of her grandmother's house. The fun began when her grandmother remembered she had a freezer full of chocolate whammy sticks. She began distributing them to neighbors and total strangers as they passed by. There were still plenty for the little girl. All she could eat.

"This," she said, "is the happiest day of my life."

On University Avenue, a twenty-year-old watched and waited.

"I always think before I move," he said. "I didn't want to be in some store when *boom!* the lights go on."

He had been thinking for himself for years: He never knew his father; his mother drank herself to death when he was a boy. By the time he was sixteen, he had been thrown out of both high school and the Job Corps. Since then he'd held just one job; it lasted three weeks. Barely paid minimum wage. He needed more than that to live. He made it hustling.

At eleven o'clock, after helping a gang open an A&P, he made a train of four shopping carts, loaded them up with groceries, and rolled them to a friend's apartment. He went back out for a stereo and a television, but the crowd on the sidewalk was rough. He got bumped, dropped the TV, and decided to quit while he was still ahead.

The bagpiper marched another thirty blocks, down to Forty-fifth Street, where he entered the north doors of the Pan Am Building and proceeded to the balcony above the main floor of Grand Central Terminal. He paused, then let go with a stirring grand finale, which echoed off the walls.

The crowd below, hundreds of people, roared.

The psychiatrist walked home humming "God Bless America."

On the steps of one of the row houses that graced the gaslit streets north of Fulton on Bed-Stuy's east side, a sixty-seven-year-old woman sat with her Putnam Avenue neighbors.

They didn't need candles, and they cursed the darkness only because it did not bring relief from the heat.

"A hundred tomorrow, they say." "Con Edison again." "You remember the last time?" "They're breaking it up on the avenue." "This is like '65 and '68 all in one." "Would you look at that?" "How could anyone have so little shame?"

The woman's neighbors took turns searching for children who were out.

They argued with children who were not but wanted to be.

Her own children came by to check on her.

They had urged her to move.

But she had lived in the three-story brick building since the 1930s, raised four children there, owned it now, had countless friends in the neighborhood, was active in the church and president of a busy block association.

Both church and block association would be busier after the blackout. There was looting in every direction, though all she and many of her neighbors saw of it was an occasional peddler selling stolen wares.

"Our instruments were our livelihoods," said one member of the Linden Woodwind Quintet. "As we walked home, up Broadway, we held on to them as if they were our lives."

The sidewalks were jammed. Kids on mopeds played chicken with cars, pedestrians, and one another. There was no music but an unsettling amount of noise.

The quintet walked up the median with their heads down, hoping if they didn't see anyone, no one would see them.

As they crossed 110th Street, with three miles behind them and three to go, their bus came over the crest of the hill. They took it to the corner of 171st and Fort Washington Avenue, where it was quiet and dark as a field in the middle of nowhere, without moon or stars.

The Harlem teenager who had thought the blackout was a bomb was shaken awake by her mother, who smelled smoke.

The teenager grabbed her baby from his crib and went to the window. Fire trucks pulled up, and firemen put out a small fire next door.

Wide awake now, she recognized the voices of boys she knew. She and her sister joined them.

They played cat and mouse with the police.

"It was a little bit scary," she said, "and a little bit fun."

At midnight the jazz trio in Windows on the World played their last song.

The staff had been taking patrons down since eleven, when Trade Center technicians got power to a service elevator with a generator. The elevator was small, the line waiting for it long; the trio's guitarist and bass took the stairs.

The band's leader waited with the restaurant staff.

He would have liked to keep playing. The musicians on the *Titanic*, he noted, had played until the ship went down. But the *Titanic*'s musicians were not bound by union regulations.

The Brownsville looter had thought of staying home after he was jumped, but he wanted more. His third foray went smoothly. The fourth was spoiled by the arrival of the police. He left Pitkin for Utica Avenue. But there, instead of simply stealing, people were "tearing up" and "burning."

He returned to an apartment crammed with people. It looked like a party, but no one was having fun. Friends and relatives were missing. Everyone was sniffing for smoke.

"I know you're not going back outside," his mother said.

"No," he said, "I'm not."

People without radios in neighborhoods without looting knew nothing about it.

Early on, people with radios didn't necessarily know more.

Reporters rushed out, but not into the neighborhoods with

widespread looting. Some would not have known how to get there.

After hearing a WINS news anchor report that New Yorkers were displaying the same aplomb they had in 1965, a Brooklyn fire chief called the radio station. "Bushwick is burning," he said.

"Where's that?" the reporter asked.

Aware that the blackout might be a political opportunity disguised as a disaster, the mayor's closest political advisers followed him to City Hall and joined commissioners in deliberations large (should he ask the governor to send the National Guard?) and small (should he appear before cameras in work clothes or dress clothes?).

At twelve-thirty a.m., the mayor held his third press conference in three hours. He was animated, even upbeat. The floodlight was blinding and hot. He reveled in it.

"This has to be your greatest campaign stunt yet," a reporter said.

"You couldn't buy this attention," the deputy mayor admitted.

A few minutes later, the fire department removed the generator that powered the light. It was needed at the city morgue.

Sometime after one a.m., the missing divorcée "pranced" around the corner. Her friend, who had been standing in front of the bar for three hours, said nothing, afraid that if she said what she was thinking she would lose her ride back to New Jersey.

Newsday began printing the *Daily News*, but the drivers' union, which was fighting with management over labor representation, balked at the idea of delivering papers printed at *Newsday*'s plant.

———

A Harlem man walked down Eighth Avenue on his way from his mother's to his girlfriend's.

He saw fireworks, smelled smoke; heard gunfire, people laughing, people crying, people cursing looters, people egging them on.

He just walked. He hadn't given up "wheeling and dealing" so he could go to jail for stealing. Since going straight, he was on a roll: First he found a job dealing blackjack at the House of Games; then, on the eve of 7/7/77, he put five dollars on 654 and won eight grand. He'd already rented rooms for a casino of his own.

His mother was safe. His girlfriend was safe. But he was too excited to sit down, let alone sleep.

He walked over to the rooms he'd rented, thinking back to '68.

Come morning, he'd furnish the rooms, cheap.

"I must look pretty good to you about now, huh, Sanchez," said a punch-drunk pulmonologist at Bellevue at about two a.m. He'd been bagging the young man for nearly four hours.

Relief came when colleagues dug several old respirators out of deep storage and carried them up sixteen flights. An "ingenious" respiratory therapist figured out how to power them the old-fashioned way, with compressed air.

By early morning, thousands of police officers were making hundreds of arrests an hour. They drove suspects to dark or dimly lit stations, but they couldn't stick around to take fingerprints and mug shots, file formal complaints, and transfer prisoners to court for their arraignments. The cops they'd left on the streets still needed assistance.

Cells filled up, then lobbies and hallways, even offices, every inch of floor.

And by the time officers returned a second or third time, it was not easy for them to remember whom they had arrested, when they had arrested them, and what they had arrested them for.

New York Times reporters finished their stories and, together with their editors, dictated copy and headlines to colleagues in Hackensack. *Record* printers set the type and (following instructions from New York) pasted up pages A and B: seven articles and a note to readers in which editors explained the paper's unusual format.

At one a.m. word had spread among passengers on the 9:20 to Manhasset that a diesel was on the way. Power diverted from Long Island arrived first. Shortly after two, the lights came back on. Passengers cheered. The lights went off. Passengers jeered. But the train began to move, slowly, toward Manhasset.

"I'm caught in a *M*A*S*H* nightmare and can't wake up," said a brawny nurse standing in Brooklyn Jewish Hospital's parking lot at three a.m. Sirens and burglar alarms sounded on Eastern Parkway and Franklin Avenue. His arms and blue smock were covered with blood.

One nurse hoisted a teenager onto a litter, located a one-and-a-half-inch gash in his head, and began to shave it. Another swabbed the blood and searched for glass. A doctor disinfected and anesthetized, then sewed five stitches. One nurse snipped; another swabbed and applied a bandage. The boy stepped down. Another took his place.

The emergency room had filled up moments after the lights went out. Nurses and orderlies moved patients to pallets in the hospital courtyard. Then the courtyard filled up, and nurses and orderlies moved patients to the cafeteria. When the hospital's backup generator failed, firemen mounted high-intensity spots on two trucks and a station wagon, thereby transforming the parking lot into a field hospital. The station wagon doubled as a supply closet.

"I've seen a lot of things in my career," said the president of the hospital's medical staff. "But never anything like this." Earlier in the evening, he had delivered a baby. "The nurse held my penlight and I went to work. It was an ordinary delivery." He no longer remembered if it had been a boy or a girl.

At four a.m., an NBC News assistant arrived at his Rockefeller Center office. Six hours earlier, his train from Philadelphia had stopped short in Newark. Six hours to travel the final fifteen miles, including two through the Lincoln Tunnel. Not bad, he thought, considering that he had walked.

"We cried," said the co-owner of Alec Zander, a Bronx furniture store. "We laughed. We wanted to kill. We just don't know what to do. We're finished."

He stood with his partner in their Grand Concourse store. It was half past four. There was a parking meter on the floor but not much more. Looters had cleaned out the basement as well as the showroom, forty bedroom sets.

His partner had driven in from Rockland County at midnight, with his shotgun. The co-owner was already there, with his.

At one point his partner darted into the street and started grabbing people. "If my partner hadn't prevented me," he said, "I would have shot some."

The *Times* people piled back into the truck and drove the finished pages to Carlstadt.

By four, the presses were running.

By five, nearly half a million copies of the late city edition were on their way to newsstands and home-delivery dealers.

Never before had the *Times* printed an entire paper on an offset press.

Shortly after five, the mayor climbed onto a table at police headquarters and met with reporters, many of whom had attended his twelve-thirty and one-thirty news conferences and then had accompanied him on a short tour of the East Side, which included stops at a hospital, a firehouse, and a few intersections.

There weren't any surprises: The mayor blamed Con Edison for the blackout, reminded people that 911 was only for emergencies, and urged them not to drive into Manhattan.

He then returned to Gracie Mansion for a nap, a shower, and a shave.

Negotiations between the *News* and its drivers' union went nowhere. Management threatened to seek damages in court. Deliver the paper yourselves, the union said. Managers did. Forty thousand copies, mostly in Queens.

On University Avenue in the Bronx, an unemployed auto mechanic, thirty-two years old, sat in his car, on the lookout for trouble.

Earlier, he had been part of the trouble.

He didn't start it, but as soon as a crowd got into the act, he joined in. People began "copping stuff out of a grocery store that was still open." Then a supermarket on Featherbed Lane, "filling shopping carts and baby carriages. After that there was no way to keep us out of an open store." Those reluctant to loot bought merchandise from looters, or gathered goods that looters had dropped or discarded.

The mechanic's take included Pampers, baby food, meat, rice, cereal, three televisions, and a case of soap. He planned to sell two of the televisions and the soap.

When he was done, he joined neighbors in front of the supermarket on the ground floor of the building where he lived with his girlfriend and their two children and, sometimes, two children from a previous marriage.

He pulled his car up on the sidewalk. "If that building goes, I have no place for my family to live."

11

Merchants and police had the first say, but in no time, countless others got into the fray.

"They are jackals, that's why," said a city councilman who represented a heavily looted Brooklyn neighborhood. "Jackals who took advantage of the darkness to destroy our stores and services."

"Why do they do it?" asked an eighteen-year-old, as if the answer were obvious. He, too, lived in a heavily looted Brooklyn neighborhood. "Got no summer jobs. That's why."

He worked in a variety store on Utica Avenue. But, he said, the looters "have nothing to do. So they come down here."

"When you see a black florist on Nostrand Avenue wiped out," and a "black-owned supermarket on the same street suffer the same fate . . . how can I buy excuses that no jobs and poverty motivated this mob action?" asked a state assemblyman from Brooklyn. "It is vandalism. Vandalism. And we can't coddle or pamper acts of vandalism."

"When you are hungry and you haven't worked in a long time . . . and the opportunity presents itself, you know it's wrong, but you take it," said an East Harlem community leader. "People who are working don't need to steal."

"When you're hungry, you're hungry," said the East Village activist.

The looters, he said, were not hungry. If they were, they would not have waited for the lights to go out to "rebel."

He was a former radical who went into party politics to embarrass concessions out of the system. He believed in confrontation and protest. But the looting was "not a protest, just a bunch of clowns," many of them hustlers and junkies, going "inside the crowd," egging it on, "taking advantage of the situation to benefit themselves."

"They don't have no chance out here," said the leader of an East Harlem gang, who spent the night trying to keep his members off the street. "So when they see the opportunity, they take it."

"In emergencies, people do what they do in everyday life," said a sociologist.

Crime was up dramatically since 1965; the looters were probably "thieves and vandals. The looting should not be thought of as a change in people but [as] a change in opportunity."

"Black teenage unemployment . . . is twice what it was a decade ago," said a Manhattan state senator. "The family income level disparity between Blacks and whites has steadily worsened, and as many Blacks are unemployed today as during the days of the Great Depression. We have systematically sowed the seeds of despair and in so doing have cultivated chaos."

"Godlessness," said a Long Island woman. "Ever since the late 1960s, when we had leaders from the president on down who forgot that they were under God and the Ten Commandments, there has been this feeling of anything goes. Nixon was pardoned and sent to San Clemente instead of being tried, convicted, and sent to jail. Eventually the trouble trickles down. And people think: If he can get away with it, why shouldn't I."

"God" gave "poor people their bread" said a member of another street gang, the Savage Skulls. "The poor people only want the same things the cops have: TVs, nice furniture, shit like that. And food. People have to eat."

"I don't think it had much to do with the loot," said a Bedford-Stuyvesant social worker who had passed the hours on her stoop with her husband and neighbors, talking and drinking beer. Although new to the neighborhood, she and her husband were already active in their block association; they were trying to figure out what to do about the boys who loitered at the top of the subway stairs, harassing people and occasionally snatching a purse.

She thought of the looters as she thought of those boys. They were angry, "getting back" at people. When she listened to their talk, she heard a lot of "I hate whitey." She understood the anger—storekeepers often treated her "like dirt." But not the hate. "They've got no skills; they can't read or write; they don't know how to do anything. All they know how to do is hate."

12

Thursday morning was many different mornings, just as the night without lights had been many different nights.

One woman, rising before the sun, stuck her head out her bedroom window.

Never before, she said, had the street been so quiet.

Nor the sky—in Queens!—so full of stars.

A twenty-two-year-old who hadn't been to bed decided the best way to save food from spoiling was to eat it.

Hours earlier, others with the same idea had set up grills on sidewalks, terraces, and fire escapes; in tiny fenced-in yards and sweeping riverfront parks.

He set his up in a Bushwick alley.

A neighbor, who had been to the butcher, brought steaks. The cook's brother, who had been to the hardware store, brought a screwdriver, to flip them.

"The new sign is the fist with a towel wrapped around it," said the cook, raising his bloody, bandaged right hand. "That's the power salute. This time it was flashlights, not guns. All power to the looters."

The men of Ladder Company 26 watched the sunrise from the rooftop of a burning Harlem building. On their way back to the firehouse (for the first time since the lights went out), they stopped for groceries. Two men went in, but the pickings were slim: two jars of gefilte fish, the only food looters had left on the shelves.

In rooms on both sides of that alley, people who had managed to fall asleep rose with a muddy mixture of despair and relief.

The grocery store, the pharmacy, and the five-and-ten were gone.

Scores of neighbors would be without jobs.

But their homes had been spared, and the smoke that woke them was from a barbecue in the alley.

With backup power still out at Bellevue, patients cheered the day's first light. They drank warm fruit juice, ate dry cereal, and waited their turn for the pay phone in the hallway, eager to let family and friends know they'd survived the night.

Lab technicians, as agitated as the patients were calm, searched storage closets and cabinets for an old microscope, the kind illuminated by ambient light and mirror instead of built-in lamp. Their great fear was that frozen specimens, essential for both diagnosis and research, would defrost before they'd had a chance to examine them.

Two young doctors hustled down stairs with flashlights, a plastic tube, and a jug. The generator they were using to power an aspirator, an electrocardiogram, and a portable X-ray camera was nearly out of gasoline. They intended to siphon a gallon out of a car.

Empire State Building staff carried breakfast up to the three dozen people who had spent the night on the observation deck. Afterward, they offered to escort anyone who wanted to walk down eighty-six still-dark flights. A few walked; most decided to wait for the elevator, though no one could tell them just how long that wait would be.

———

In the lobby of the Statler Hilton, where two hundred people without reservations had spent the night, two hotel guests tiptoed to the side of a young woman who was crying.

Shaking off a few hours' sleep, she had just discovered that her boyfriend of the night before was gone, and her wallet was missing.

The man and woman, who had been up all night helping the hotel staff, asked her where she lived, walked her to the street, hailed a cab, and paid the fare.

"Why, we're from Louisiana, honey," one of them explained to a reporter who asked about their largesse. "We're used to trouble. If I had a daughter, I'd want somebody to do it for her."

Two men stood outside a Columbus Avenue café, their tired eyes trained on the street.

All night long, gangs had swarmed up and down the avenue.

No one came near them.

Each of them carried a shotgun.

"I was determined," the owner said, "to shoot the first mother that put his hands on my property."

A Far Rockaway man stumbled through the rubble of his East Harlem store and thought back, almost longingly, to the riots of 1968, the night Ray killed King.

That, in retrospect, was nothing. Looters took a hundred suits. The following day he and his brothers installed a solid metal sliding door, like a garage door; the day after that, they were back in business.

This time looters took everything but two straw hats and a few rolls of toilet paper. What they didn't take, they destroyed.

"They didn't have to break that," he said, pointing to a mirror. "That's just malicious. They're trying to tell me something. Well, they got their message across."

———

The owner of Gramercy Park Hardware arrived early, grabbed a poster board and marker, and went to work on a new sign.

BUY IT NOW: BATTERIES, FLASHLIGHTS, CANDLES. STOCK UP.

He sold three thousand candles before noon.

On Watkins Street, near the corner of Belmont in the Brownsville section of Brooklyn, a decorator sat in his shop trying to fill some orders.

It wasn't easy.

He was working alone. (His sewing-machine operator and his presser had been unable to get to Brownsville.)

And without much light. (Having seen looters on Pitkin— young men making their way down the avenue with mattresses and box springs on top of their heads—he had left the steel shutter pulled down over his showroom window.)

Every few minutes the phone rang. It was his wife, urging him to close and come home.

Finally, he did.

The looters were gone, but so were the shutters, windows, and doors.

The owner of a West Side deli left Valley Stream, Long Island, in the dark, not knowing what he was going to find. He made great time, and as he neared the Queensboro Bridge, the light of the rising sun struck the tops of the tallest skyscrapers and began to climb down, creating the illusion that all over Manhattan, at that very moment, the power was being restored.

It wasn't, but he arrived to find his deli as he had left it, and not long after he arrived, the power on his block was restored.

"This may sound corny," he said, "but . . . we felt like God was just ahead of us all the way. And it was all over."

13

As anyone with the nerve to ask quickly discovered, looters had lots to say about the looting.

"Being that the lights are out," one young looter said, "and the niggers are going hungry, we're going to take what we want, and what we want is what we need."

"I've got three kids and I don't have no job," said another. He had stolen a stereo, a dining room set, bedroom furniture, tennis shoes, and some jewelry. Worth $3,000 in all, he thought.

He said he'd had the opportunity to rob. So he robbed.

"I'd do it again."

"We're poor," said a nineteen-year-old father of two, "and this is our way of getting rich."

"Prices have gone too high," said a man in Bushwick, "now we're going to have no prices. When we get done, there ain't going to be no more Broadway."

"Why us, man?" one of the owners of LeMans asked two of the looters in his store.

It didn't make sense. Like the looters, he and his partner were black men. They sold stylish clothes to black men.

"Your things were too high, man," one of the looters said.

"Your 'bourgie' customers drive up in their Mercedes," said

the other, "and they think we're shit because we ain't got nothing. Well, we are getting something."

"Listen," a looter said to a radio reporter who had asked him
if he knew that what he was doing was wrong. "There are folks
around here who ain't never had a decent suit of clothes. Well,
tonight they are going to get it."

"You take your chance when you get your chance," said a
Brooklyn man in his thirties, holding a wine bottle in one hand
and a television in the other.

"It gets dark here every night," said a teenager who had just
helped empty the shelves of a drugstore. "Every night stores get
broke into, every night people get mugged, every night you get
scared on the street. But nobody pays no attention until a blackout comes."

"Why?" a reporter asked a looter in East Harlem.
"Why not?" the looter said.

14

On 138th Street in the Bronx, the blackout wasn't over. Not even Con Edison knew when it would be, and if (as that West Side deli owner thought) God were around, He or She was, as always, on the side of the heaviest battalions.

Four or five hundred people, most of them young, followed the first light of day through the window of the National Shoe Store. Three police cars pulled up. Officers piled out wearing riot helmets and carrying clubs. Some of the looters fled.

Several blocks to the east, between Willis Avenue and Cypress, smaller groups streamed in and out of supermarkets, pawnshops, liquor, jewelry, and appliance stores. Police arrived, but looters had cover from neighbors on the rooftops, flinging rocks, bottles, and bricks. Only after they had closed the street and cleared the rooftops could the police get close enough to scare some of the looters away.

"Twenty businesses have been wiped out in this neighborhood," one detective said. "It's just like war."

The seventeen-year-old in the Harlem high-rise woke from a couple of hours' sleep to find that the power was still out. Her friends and neighbors were still out, too.

She woke her sister, and they joined them.

"Now," the seventeen-year-old said, "we could see what was there and get what we wanted."

They stayed out until store owners began to arrive half an

hour later, and brought home detergent, baby food, and a case of spinach.

My only hope is my security, thought a New Rochelle man as he approached the four-story furniture and appliance store he managed on Third Avenue at 117th Street.

He'd installed a sound detector, a noise detector, and a camera, all backed up by batteries and the Holmes Detective Agency.

The alarm had sounded, and Holmes had come with dogs. But looters had already helped themselves to 155 television sets and every piece of furniture that a few men working together could carry.

The manager, a former Third Avenue store owner himself, had come out of retirement to manage the store, Grand Union Furniture, when its owner, an old friend, moved to Puerto Rico.

He pulled up as close to the store as he could get.

There were hundreds of people in the street.

"What really hurt me," he said, were the "looks on their faces. Like it was a big joke. . . . This sounds terrible, I know, but the way I feel, the goddamn policemen should have shot a couple of those. . . . Why would they just let them loot and put people out of business?"

On Pitkin Avenue, in Brownsville, the supermarket shelves were empty, as were the appliance showrooms, and the camera- and jewelry-store displays.

The looting had slowed to a trickle.

A couple of children wandered out of a bargain store with pads and pencils, followed by a woman with pots and pans.

Two women pushed baby carriages loaded with rockers, toys, diapers, baby bottles, and baby food out of a children's store.

Broken glass covered the sidewalk like old city snow.

Where it had spilled into the gutters, the water running from fire hydrants to sewers ran red with the blood of the first looters.

On West 110th Street in Manhattan, looters streamed in and out of the battered door of an appliance store.

"Shopping," said one middle-aged woman, "with no money required."

Half a mile south, the co-owner of a Columbus Avenue furniture store told reporters how his employees, armed only with buckets and water, had done their best but ultimately failed to keep looters away.

"I just don't know what to do," he said, turning toward slashed couches and smashed chandeliers. "I am not a gun man. I don't own one, and I wouldn't know how to use one if I did have one. But I can't even get the private security agencies on the phone and I know the cops won't be able to guard the store. They have a lot of other things to do. People like me have to get help. Disaster aid, or something."

Thirteen years earlier, a loan from the Small Business Administration, its second loan ever to minority businessmen, had helped him and his partner get started.

Perhaps the SBA would help again.

"If we don't get help, we're wiped out."

In addition to a few fires and scattered looting, a WINS radio reporter sent to central Harlem after a night in the studio observed an odd exuberance. "People were grabbing shirts, pairs of pants, anything, and running around, and laughing. . . . It was as if they were suddenly free."

At one point, two men approached him.

"How much is that tape recorder worth?" one asked.

"Supposing we grabbed it," the other said.

"Then I wouldn't be able to tell people what's going on up here."

"Yeah, that's true," the first man said, and they walked away.

On the Grand Concourse at Fordham Road, two looters on their way out of an appliance store were startled by the sight of two men in sport jackets and ties.

They dropped the boxes they were carrying and froze.

But they had no reason to worry.

The men in sport jackets were from Con Edison, a property protection foreman and a member of his staff. The only theft they cared about was the theft of electricity—customers, usually business customers, monkeying with their meters or tapping in to someone else's lines, taking the utility for tens of millions of dollars a year.

They had arrived at their Kingsbridge Avenue office early and (with no electricity to protect) wandered over to see what was going on. They watched small groups of men, slowed only by the throng in the streets, pull up in El Caminos and Rancheros and hit one store after another as if according to a carefully orchestrated plan. The windows of the supermarket had been bricked up since 1968; several men went through the roof. Only the Crazy Eddie was spared: The manager stood in the door with a shotgun and a white German shepherd.

The Con Edison men returned to their office.

The looters picked up their boxes and walked away.

As two jewelers, husband and wife, surveyed the damage to their Bushwick store, a small boy approached them.

"It's our Christmas," he said. "Give me something."

Late morning, the manager of Grand Union Furniture and several employees were cleaning up.

An armed guard stood by.

Two men walked in and picked up a washing machine.

The guard drew his gun.

"You either kill me," one of the looters said, "or I go out the door with the washer."

The guard looked at the manager, then put the gun away.

The two men went out the door with the washer.

15

People agreed that there was a reason.

But they disagreed vehemently about what that reason was.

So they argued.

"Man, times are hard and it was a chance in a lifetime to get over," said a Harlem man. "There is no work for anyone. Black folks don't have much and we are kicked and stepped on every time we turn around. I feel sorry for those who got caught."

"Looting is never justified," said one of that man's neighbors. "I've been poor and raised two children and I never stole anything from anyone. I worked hard and long. Too many people feel that the world owes them a living. No one owes anyone anything."

"The only way we're going to get it is to take," said an eighteen-year-old East Harlem woman, standing on the sidewalk with her sixteen-year-old friend. "All the stores do is rip you off, taking what little money we have."

The little money she had, $52 a week, came from her job as a youth counselor.

"Puerto Ricans and niggers get the most trouble," she said.

"When they get a chance they're going to destroy, and they will take what they need. They think this is bad, they ain't seen nothing yet."

———

"My prices are competitive," said the owner of Morris Toy-land, dismissing the idea that looters had taken revenge on store owners. "In the first blackout I sold batteries for a quarter; downtown they were selling for a dollar."

His contribution to the neighborhood included hiring local people.

The "good ones" worked, as he had worked since his uncle offered him a job at thirteen. The "bad ones" didn't need work. They had money and fine clothes without it.

"When it's dark you take everything you can get," said a friend of the East Harlem youth counselor. "Look, dungarees are $17.99 and sneakers are $24. Who wants to buy sneakers for $24? Carter is not giving us what we want. He ain't giving us nothing. So we have to take it."

"They looted because for twelve years they've been pro-grammed to take," said the owner of Sylvester's, a Nostrand Avenue sporting-goods store.

Returning to his store shortly after the lights went out, he recognized many looters. He had sold them basketballs and soccer cleats. They played on one of the four Little League teams he sponsored. They'd come to him when they needed advice about school or work, or when they were having trouble with their parents. Parents came when they were having trouble with their kids.

When the looters in his store saw him, they looked as if they wished it were even darker than it was.

He'd heard people say looters were getting back at merchants.

His customers had no grounds for complaint. His merchandise was top-quality, and he always sold his sneakers for $1 less than the $15 they'd pay in the department stores downtown.

"More is expected of a black store owner," he said. "You're expected to be more compassionate; you can't sell shoddy goods. And if a bill comes to $18.25, you're expected to forget the 25 cents."

Moral decline, that's what it was. "The news media and the social workers" contributed to it, and though it was hardly limited to black people, his concern was for blacks. "We're getting away from the merit syndrome. There was a time a black had to be four times as good as everyone else to get something. Now he thinks that just because he is, he gets it."

"It was an opportunity for me to get some food and maybe make a little money," said the unemployed auto mechanic who, after a few hours of looting, had passed the early morning protecting his University Avenue building from other looters.

"Most of the people around here don't have money and jobs. When something like this goes down, even an honest man would steal."

"Jobs?" asked the thirty-four-year-old owner of a Bedford-Stuyvesant boutique, indignantly.

The looters had robbed twenty-five locals of their jobs when they sacked Spinners, the only supermarket in the neighborhood. They had robbed her three employees of their jobs.

"These are just people in the neighborhood who took advantage of an opportunity and broke into stores and destroyed other black people's lives."

"I think a lot of it was just mass hysteria," said the sixty-seven-year-old woman who lived on Putnam Avenue. "Someone started it, and it was just follow-the-leader after that." A lot of them were the "same kind of people who go on relief and feel the world owes them something." One woman came walking down the street with a baby carriage full of stolen goods for sale. "It's one thing to steal something, but then to just walk down the street parading it in a baby carriage!

"I don't know how her conscience would let her do it."

"If you didn't jump in when the lights went off, you didn't get nothing," said a sixteen-year-old, showing off a pair of pants with the price tag still on. "If you're slow, you blow. The people out here looting at five in the morning were the last of the scavengers. There was nothing left by that time.

"Everybody was out getting theirs. I wanted to get mine."

"Attitudes have changed," said the police department's deputy chief inspector. "Each year people are doing more illegal things and paying for them less."

The police aren't shooting.

The courts are too crowded to administer justice.

"There is no fear of . . . physical punishment. There is no humiliation in being arrested" or known as a thief. "Disrespect for the law has grown."

People should know better, but don't.

"Everyone says they should know better," said the director of the East Harlem Community Corporation, speaking to a *Washington Post* reporter.

The director had watched the destruction of upper Third Avenue.

He knew many of the looters, kids in their twenties.

They'd been in jail, never had a job, and they weren't going to get one now. The government said unemployment was at 15 percent, but it was twice that, and twice that again for the young. The last time anyone had counted, four out of ten families were on welfare, and that wasn't counting the sick and the old.

Whites had fled the neighborhood. Now they—and many black people, too—said the looters should know better.

Why?

"If you're saving money to go to school or something, then you're making sacrifices and you have a goal."

What about someone with no goal and no alternative?

"Their attitude is that the system is rotten and it owes me this. They're going to rob and rip off to eat and survive."

"I hope you out-of-town people tell it like it is," said a Bedford-Stuyvesant police sergeant to the same *Washington Post* reporter, who thought it worth noting that he was a black man.

"The lights went out. A bunch of greedy people took advantage. Plain and simple. Don't go with all that sociological bullshit."

"They saw this as a chance to get that pair of slacks or TV set that they couldn't afford," a spokesman for the sergeant's precinct told another reporter.

Few of those arrested in the 81st were hardened criminals.

"I am not condoning it. It's wrong, and people should be arrested for it. But what happened here was a spontaneous act." It was a hot night, and people were out on the streets. The city went "totally dark. What do you expect in an area with high unemployment among adults and teenagers?"

Outside the precinct house, Bedford-Stuyvesant residents sided with the sergeant. They had seen people of all ages, people with jobs and without, people they saw in church on Sunday.

"The problem," said one woman, born and raised in Brooklyn, "was character and morals."

"A lot of people saw things they've never had before," said a man on Linden Boulevard. He was carrying tennis sneakers and a pair of pants.

"It's like a twinkling in front of their eyes. Most of the people are on welfare. They can't afford to buy."

Behind him, a row of buildings burned.

"What about the fires?" a reporter asked him.

"Probably everybody out here owes money to these stores," he said. "If you destroy them, then you destroy the records."

Sure enough, the sidewalk beneath their feet was covered with file cards, ledgers, and receipts.

In 1965, nothing like this happened, said a radio commentator, a former governor of California.

In a "matter of twelve years," civilization had come "unglued."

"Social spending has been reduced dramatically," said Robert Wagner, Jr., who was New York's mayor in 1965.

"That year, the city spent $100 million on programs for youth in deprived areas. All that is out the window now."

"People have seen Watergate felons make money on books and speeches and television appearances and lectures," said a Manhattan psychologist. "They've seen kidnappers collecting ransoms and hijackers having their demands met. Crime, it seems, does pay. People believe they can get away with murder."

A twelve-year-old Brooklyn boy said he was happy the neighborhood shoe store was looted.

Some months back he'd gone in to buy a pair of sneakers. Pro-Keds.

He was two cents short on a $13 pair.

The owner sent him away. The boy hadn't looted that store, but he'd stolen two writing pads from another.

———

"Animals," said the owner of a Harlem shoe store. "This blackout brought out the scum of the earth from our communities; they should be locked up, and the key thrown away."

"You know we weren't animals up here," said a Bronx woman, who had hoped to get two fancy pillows, $100 apiece, but settled for two rolls of linoleum for her children's room. The looting showed "how well people can work together if they have a common goal and nobody harasses them. People took their turns climbing in through the broken glass, and nobody tried to push or tried to get ahead."

Did looters think there was anything wrong with stealing? a reporter asked.

"Poor people know that all the rich people are stealing," she said.

"If there's an opportunity to commit a burglary, they commit a burglary," said a Harlem detective from his bed in Metropolitan Hospital, where he was being treated for the back injuries he had sustained in Morris Toyland.

"If there's an opportunity to score on an old lady, they do it. And if they know they can get away with it, they loot. When they are caught, they walk. So they have no respect for the law." The difference between Wednesday night and every other, he said, was simply one of degree.

"He should know," a colleague said. The detective had been a decoy cop. Mugged 104 times, with forty citations for bravery and meritorious work.

Shortly before he was called to the toy store, he had arrested half a dozen looters. He asked one why he did it.

"Because I knew the meat was going to go bad," the looter said.

"The only trouble," the detective said, "was that he was stealing a television."

With "no goddamn jobs" and "everybody on welfare," a young Brooklyn woman had no apologies.

"I feel like this," she said. "God closed out the lights for one night to let us have the opportunity to get back for all the times that we have been beat, for all the times that we have been oppressed, for all the months that we ain't got Pampers around this neighborhood for our kids' behinds.

"We got Pampers now, baby. Now we got Pampers."

"I don't blame the looters," said a Bushwick jeweler. "Society's conditions are such that these people are forced to do what they did."

He assumed his words would make other merchants cringe.

"I am not condoning the looting, mind you. But we have to provide jobs so that these kids have something to do. Otherwise they are going to keep on at this."

"I got it coming to me, man," one young looter said.

He had seven siblings, no father, and a mother who he said was interested only in booze.

"I didn't ask to be born."

16

"This is like a wake," said a Bronx merchant as he and his wife stood on the sidewalk across the street from Merchants Housewares, his Prospect Avenue general store. All morning people from the neighborhood had been stopping by to say how sorry they were, urging him not to give up on the block.

"If we had known your store was in danger," said the head of United Bronx Parents, "we would have sent someone out to guard it."

At one point a policeman handed the merchant a box. In it were a few clocks. "I think these are yours," he said.

Friends and family of Lavey Yitzhak Freedman gathered at the Lincoln Square Synagogue.

Some brought flashlights.

Some brought bagels.

Synagogue staff lit the stairways with candles, but in the sanctuary, the skylight and stained glass provided plenty of light.

The rabbi told the story of another Lavey Yitzhak, an eighteenth-century rabbi who so loved the Sukkot blessings that one year, in his enthusiasm, he put his hand right through the glass door on the case where the ritual objects, the lulav and et-rog, were stored.

The rabbi was not deterred by the glass.

The family was not deterred by the blackout.

The baby was born, seven pounds, seven ounces, on Seventy-seventh Street, on one special day: July 7, 1977.

He was circumcised on another.

The owner of Merchants had been home in bed, in Ardsley, when he received a call from his niece in Colorado. She had heard there was a blackout in New York. He thought back to 1965: strong sales of flashlights, batteries, and candles. Lots of fun.

A few minutes later, he received a frantic call from the manager of another store on the block.

He wanted to go in right away; his wife persuaded him to wait until morning.

They arrived at half past five.

The looting was over. The block was roped off. The rubble on the floor of his store was a foot high.

There was no ice.

No air-conditioning.

No water in high-rise sinks, toilets, showers, or tubs. (City water pressure allowed water to rise four or five stories; above that, people depended on pumps.)

No break in the heat wave: Each hour was hotter than the one before.

No swimming on North Shore beaches, which were closed after powerless city sewage plants dumped raw sewage into the East River and the narrows leading to Long Island Sound.

And no traffic, except on the roads to the South Shore, where hundreds of thousands of people with no work decided to spend the day.

Two hundred and fifty thousand of them ended up at Jones Beach, including a few reporters, who, fearing that neither swimming nor sunbathing was newsworthy, searched for someone who had something memorable to say. The best they could come up with was a beach blanket full of people feigning worry that their offices would be closed the following day, Friday the fifteenth. If the power weren't restored, they would have to survive the weekend unpaid.

"Merchants was my life," its owner said. "My father opened it in the 1930s; I worked there when I was a kid. My brother and I took over when we got out of the army, after the war."

What had been a fifteen-by-forty-foot rental was now ten thousand square feet of selling space and five or six thousand feet of storage. He sold housewares, hardware, paint, stationery, toys, cribs, carriages, dishes, and linens. Everything. And the building, which he now owned, was a mainstay of the block.

The block was at the intersection of Southern Boulevard, 149th Street, and Prospect Avenue, at the edge of a "very rough neighborhood." People called the precinct Fort Apache.

But, he said, "Merchants was not a ghetto store. When customers returned something, I gave them a full refund. When there was something wrong with something they bought, I took care of it. I got along well with my customers. I liked them, a lot."

Once a year there was a break-in, but he was never held up. All seven of his employees were locals.

The owners of the grocery store down the block had guarded their store with guns. He didn't own one, and he wasn't sorry.

"I wasn't going to shoot people to protect property," he said.

A young couple strolling down Lexington Avenue spotted a dozen or more men gathered outside a storefront just north of Eighty-sixth Street.

The couple knew that there had been looting up Lexington, in

Spanish Harlem, but in their neighborhood, even the parties had been subdued.

They walked a block closer, then stopped.

One of the men stepped up to the storefront and peered through the window.

He had something in his hand.

They all did.

The man backed away. Another took his place.

Some of the men were reading.

Racing forms. They were outside an offtrack betting parlor, hoping against hope that it would open before the first race.

Insurance was easier to come by than a mortgage in the South Bronx, but not by much. It had been years since private carriers insured merchants against theft. The federal government offered crime insurance, but that—$1,000 for each incident—wouldn't do much good now.

The easiest insurance to get was fire insurance.

That's why, in the small circle of merchants standing on the corner of 149th Street and Prospect Avenue that morning—a grocer, the owner of a ladies' shop, an eye doctor, the owner of a coffee shop, and the owner of Merchants—only the owner of the ladies' shop was not in mourning. In fact, he was all smiles. His store was on fire.

"I am outraged," said the mayor. "The blackout has threatened our safety and has seriously impacted our economy. We have been needlessly subjected to a night of terror in many communities that have been wantonly looted and burned."

The looters would be punished.

The city would investigate.

But a few things were already clear.

God was not responsible.

Con Edison was.

The utility's performance was "at the very least gross negligence and at the worst far more serious.

"The blackout shouldn't have happened," the mayor said.

"It happened, and we want to find out why."

17

The lights went back on at Con Edison's Union Square head-quarters shortly after three in the afternoon, and twenty minutes later, the president, the chairman, and the vice president of engineering briefed reporters.

What never happened, had happened, the president said: a rapid succession of lightning strikes, direct hits.

The first strike took out Indian Point.

The second took out two lines running south from Millwood.

The third, coming just before nine o'clock, took out two of the lines that carried electricity from upstate and New England through Pleasant Valley.

Engineers increased local generation and struggled to match supply and demand so that the spikes and deficits that followed a manageable loss of one part of the system didn't damage other parts or, worse, set in motion a cascading loss of power that would bring down the whole system. But their efforts were undermined by a fourth bolt, which took out the last remaining link to the north. The line connecting Con Edison and Long Island Lighting overloaded, and LILCO cut itself off. A few minutes later New Jersey followed suit, leaving the system wholly dependent upon one 1,000-megawatt generating plant in Ravenswood, Queens. At that point, the president said, Ravenswood was lost to its own "protective devices."

18

The sun was still high in the sky, but in Williamsburg the last looters darted in and out of the shadows of the elevated tracks.

The manager of a clothing store, standing alone on the sidewalk, watched them come and go.

One group rolled dozens of new tires, three or four to a man, down Broadway.

The power was still out.

The entire inventory of the manager's store was gone.

"This," he said, "is the end of Broadway in Brooklyn."

A few blocks north, on Graham Avenue, a man sat out in front of his pharmacy in the sun. He had a baseball bat in his lap, as did the two men who sat with him. Every now and then the pharmacist went inside to take a phone call, fill a prescription, dispense baby food and diapers (for free: It was an emergency), or arrange deliveries to people who could not or would not leave their homes. The two men, whom he had hardly known before that morning, didn't budge.

The neighborhood, the pharmacist said, was predominantly Puerto Rican, and its residents were determined to prevent the looting from spreading.

Many people came by to encourage him.

One woman brought lunch.

"The blackout," he said, "brought me closer to my neighbors."

———

The police commissioner declared a corrections state of emergency, which allowed him to skirt, for ten days, the rule (imposed a few years earlier by a federal court order) that prohibited the city from putting more than one person in one city prison cell. Then he asked a federal judge for permission to re-open the Men's House of Detention, the dilapidated twelve-story prison adjacent to the courthouse, which had been closed by another court order, in 1974. It was know as the Tombs.

He had no choice.

Every prison cell in the city was full.

Every precinct-house detention cell was full.

Every detention cell in the Manhattan, Bronx, and Brooklyn criminal courthouses was full, and on Centre Street, outside the Manhattan courthouse, the line of patrol cars, paddy wagons, police vans, and buses waiting to unload prisoners stretched for blocks. The police had told court officers to expect a thousand prisoners; there were already that many inside. In the Bronx, where the police needed every vehicle with gas in its tank on the streets, it was not vehicles lined up outside the courthouse but prisoners themselves, in 92-degree heat.

"It's a motherfucker," said a firefighter on break in Bushwick, his face painted with black soot, snot, and sweat.

Twenty-seven fires burned on Broadway alone.

"A motherfucker, when you've been fighting a fire, been up all night, maybe eighteen hours now, and you know the prick that lit this job is across the street laughing at you and probably torching another joint."

Most stores were closed, as were most offices, and many deli and restaurant owners, like every ice-cream vendor, were giving away food that would soon spoil. For every dollar lost in revenue, the city (and state) lost its share in taxes. To add insult to injury, the merchants who did make a killing that day—in their apartments and in the basements of their apartment buildings, in abandoned apartments and storefronts, in alleys, on sidewalks, and right out in the middle of the walking malls that they and their neighbors made of many streets—made that killing tax-free.

They unloaded clothing, footwear, and food, especially baby food, as fast as if they had been giving it away, but they sold everything that was priced right by the end of the day.

"You got people out here selling thirty-dollar sneakers for ten dollars," said the Brownsville looter. "You going to tell me people aren't going to buy thirty-dollar sneakers for ten dollars? Everybody would."

In addition to sneakers, the looter sold jewelry, portable stereos, and a color television, everything but four other televisions, which he lost when a neighbor discovered his cache and called the police.

Even without the televisions, he grossed $2,000, which, as soon as it reopened, he planned to put in the bank.

In and around the Brooklyn Criminal Courthouse, there was chaos the likes of which people who had been doing business there since the Depression had never seen. Hundreds of prisoners stood shoulder to shoulder, face-to-face, in a few small holding cells, while their friends and relatives (and the friends and relatives of people who were missing and assumed, by their families, to be prisoners) stood shoulder to shoulder, face-to-face, in the lobby and out on the courthouse steps.

It was hot on the steps, hotter in the lobby, and hottest in the cells.

The lights were still out, and not a single prisoner had been arraigned.

The Brownsville decorator sat with his wife on the front porch of their Malverne home.

The phone rang. They were afraid to pick it up. But it was their son, not bad news from Brownsville.

He pleaded. Dad, move the shop elsewhere, anywhere but that neighborhood.

"How can I?" the decorator asked. "I own the building. I could not find such good help, or move my equipment and fabrics. I have been in this one place all of my working life."

His son didn't argue. He simply said, "Dad, I know you can find a way."

"The air is fresh," said the manager of an Upper East Side bicycle store, ticking off the reasons why this day was among his favorites in New York, ever:

"I can hear birds.

"And a cricket, I heard a cricket in New York City.

"And last night. I could see the stars."

19

After brief statements, the three Con Edison executives took questions.

"Aren't cables protected from lightning?" a reporter asked the vice president of engineering.

"Yes," he said. "The topmost wire running on the tower is a lightning arrestor. Perhaps the lightning bolt was of an unusual shape."

"The mayor has charged you with gross negligence and ordered an investigation. Do you have any comment on that?"

"That's conviction before trial," said the chairman.

"Was Con Edison incompetent?"

"No," all three said at the same time.

"Who was the engineer at the Control Center?"

They refused to give his name.

"He is a highly experienced professional," said the vice president of engineering. He was "honestly trying to protect Con Edison customers from inconvenience. . . . The fellow feels terrible; he feels, rightly or wrongly, that he let somebody down."

"It was," the vice president said, a "trillion-to-one shot."

"You said the power would be restored in a few hours six hours ago, and six hours before that. Why is it taking so long?"

Engineers and technicians had to check the entire system for damage, the vice president said, and they had to do most of that checking on-site, at scores of locations, from power plants to substations to vaults under city streets and sidewalks. They had to reset tripped circuit breakers manually, then reenergize all the high-voltage lines. But miles of those lines were underground lines, insulated and cooled by oil under high pressure. The oil pressure came from pumps that were powered by the main system. When the system went down, the oil pressure dropped, and it would take electricity and time to build it back up.

Once they had checked the system for damage, reset circuit breakers, and restored oil pressure, engineers could begin to restore power. But even then they had to do it slowly, one neighborhood at a time, starting with those adjacent to generators or substations.

The vice president said that engineers had already restored a third of the system, including most of Queens and Westchester, and significant parts of Manhattan and Staten Island. The remainder of Staten Island would be next, followed by all of Brooklyn, the remainder of Manhattan, and finally the Bronx, which got its power by way of Manhattan.

20

On Broadway in Bushwick, hundreds of people remained in the streets. Some played music. Some danced to it. Some sold stolen goods—batteries were going for $2 apiece. Some bought them. Some looted. Some scavenged for loot others had discarded or dropped. One group of kids rummaged through a pile of sneakers, trying to make pairs. One man wrestled with the trunk of his car. He had packed it with several bloody sides of beef and couldn't close it. For an entire block, the sidewalk between him and the butcher shop was covered with fresh pigs' feet.

The power came back on.

A minute later, police arrived in riot gear.

Word spread that they weren't wearing name tags.

A sure sign, people said, that trouble was about to begin.

A *Village Voice* reporter asked a cop why he wasn't wearing a name tag. The cop said he lost his.

Another said he didn't "fucking feel like wearing" a badge.

Sure enough, one group of officers charged into a crowd that had entered a shoe store near Linden Avenue.

Swinging nightsticks.

The power went back off.

Members of the street gang called Savage Skulls gathered nearby. They carried sticks of their own and threatened revenge if the cops didn't behave.

The corrections commissioner led reporters on a tour of the detention pens in the Manhattan Criminal Courthouse.

Prisoners called out. "I am innocent," more than one said.

They pleaded with reporters to phone relatives on their behalf.

One man said he'd been arrested after he picked up a bag of Pampers on the sidewalk outside a grocery store. The police had separated him from his two-year-old son. The boy was wearing a chain and medallion around his neck. The man was worried someone would try to grab it.

"I had to learn to deal with the element in a way they required," said a forty-one-year-old Crown Heights man, who had planted himself behind the counter of his Bushwick pharmacy shortly after the lights went out. He had not budged since.

"I don't say it proudly. I have children and I try to raise them decently. I go to church. I don't like doing it, but it's a must. . . . If you capitulate, forget it, they'll walk right over you."

He had bought the place in 1970 from two white men. For a year he had a partner, a third white man. But there were ugly scenes in the store; half a dozen times a year, they were robbed. The thieves came in every door, down through the ceiling, up through the floor. When they stripped his partner's car right in front of his eyes, the man sold his share of the business and quit. "It was too much to ask of a human being to stay."

Four years earlier, he'd had nine employees; now he had three, and a pistol.

Late Thursday afternoon, nineteen hours into his vigil, he left to get something to eat. When he returned half an hour later, looters, looking like professional movers, were emptying the place.

They had entered through a side window.

He fired shots over their heads, and they fled.

Most of his merchandise was gone.

Looters would be punished harshly, said the mayor.

Looters are already being punished, said a Legal Aid attorney:

Dozens of them have been crammed into airless eight-by-twelve-foot holding cells intended for a few prisoners and short stays. Those conditions, he added, would be intolerable for any prisoner. But these people have not even been charged with a crime.

The chair of the city commission charged with overseeing corrections agreed that the prisoners were merely suspects; they had rights.

But he understood the mayor's anger.

"Committing a crime during an emergency," he said, "is the ultimate disrespect for the law. It's not like stealing a grapefruit from the corner store."

Shortly before six, a crowd entered an appliance warehouse at Stone Avenue and Somers Street in the Ocean Hill section of Brooklyn.

Moments later, the warehouse was empty and on fire.

By the time firemen arrived, the flames had spread in two directions, igniting two houses behind it and four tenements, home to twenty families, across the street. Forty-five minutes later, the building collapsed.

A man who lived nearby said that a looter, angry after a cop smacked him, started it with gasoline.

By early Thursday evening, police had either recovered or identified half the cars stolen from Ace Pontiac. Some had been stripped, some wrapped around trees and telephone poles by thieves who, like many New Yorkers, didn't know how to drive.

Few merchants had lost as much, but the owner was looking on the bright side. He had recently transferred most of his stock to a showroom on Fordham Road. The stolen cars were insured, and Detroit had already promised to replace them.

"How could looters drive fifty new cars away undetected?" a reporter asked him.

"This is Fort Apache and the cops had their hands full. I'm

cool. . . . I'm used to it after so many years. What can I tell you? I'm healthy."

Brooklyn was the last stop on the mayor's five-borough black-out tour.

It had been a long day, but not a particularly challenging one. With aides at his side, he had repeatedly lashed out at two ills—crime and Con Edison—that, in the words of one clever observer, rated just behind cancer in the public eye.

But the mayor wasn't all gloom and doom. In Bushwick and Bedford-Stuyvesant, he praised the young people who had helped sanitation workers begin to clean up Broadway. He praised the residents who had reported sales and stashes of loot to the police. He praised the clergymen and community leaders who, at that very moment, were driving around their neighborhoods with bullhorns, urging people to stay off the streets.

The looting, he said, was over.

All but one fire, in Ocean Hill, was out.

Fewer than fifty thousand people in two neighborhoods—one of which was Yorkville, his own—were without power.

Most people had risen to the occasion. He was grateful, and once again proud to be a New Yorker.

A reporter asked him about the city council president's visit to a power substation in Buchanan. After talking with employees there, none of whom had seen lightning, the city council president had concluded that God had absolutely nothing to do with the blackout.

"Has he reported to you on that?" the reporter asked.

"Who?" the mayor asked in jest.

The mayor admitted that his first name was Abraham.

But he insisted he was not in the habit of speaking with God.

21

The argument in the streets began with the merchants and the police; the argument in the newspapers began with the editors of *The New York Times*.

In an editorial that appeared just hours after the power was restored, the paper praised the citizenry for its indomitable spirit; the police for their remarkable restraint; and the mayor for his leadership. They wished he had withheld his indictment of Con Edison until all the facts were in, but they themselves wanted to know why, despite all the changes that Con Edison had made since 1965, the system had failed again.

The social question was the same as the electrical: Why?

Despite the widespread analogies to the November 1965 blackout, the "appropriate analogy" was to the riots of the 1960s, which began a few months before the November blackout, in Harlem and Bedford-Stuyvesant.

Most of the looting took place in poor neighborhoods, or in the poorest pockets of mixed neighborhoods, like Manhattan's Upper West Side.

Most of those arrested were young black and Hispanic males.

The improvements to the electrical system had not been matched by improvements to the social system, the editors wrote. In fact, for the poorest New Yorkers, "not much" had changed.

Prospects for employment had "steadily worsened."

The rules weren't working. "Under stress" or "exceptional circumstances," the poor saw "no reason to play by those rules."

22

Friday morning. Merchants swept, shoveled, and dragged debris out to the street.

They took photographs for insurance, if they had insurance.

They calculated losses, which in most instances was easy: everything.

And they thought aloud about what they were going to do now.

Those inclined to stay replaced plate glass with plate glass, or with plywood while they waited for the glass man.

Those inclined to quit put up wood for good.

As always, there were exceptions.

"I'm putting glass back in the window to hold a clearance sale," said the owner of what, for twenty-seven years, had been Superior Furniture, in the Bronx. "But I'm not going to come back in."

With the help of the police, he'd saved his books, but he lost his entire showroom, five rooms of furniture and appliances—including forty of forty-four glass chandeliers—$80,000 worth of merchandise, "good merchandise, beautifully set up.

"I've had enough. I'm going to quit. I'll do something else. Leave the neighborhood to the sharpies."

"I'm responsible for twenty-five families," said the owner of the Radio Clinic. "The families of the people who work for me."

He had watched the looting of his Broadway store from the median before a looter chased him away.

"What's going to happen to them if I pull out?

"As bad as I got hit, there are other guys who got wiped out. What's going to happen if they can't reopen? What can the city and the government do to keep people like us from leaving these neighborhoods?"

Loans. There was talk of loans from the Small Business Administration, which had already declared the city a small-business disaster area. Up to $250,000, depending on the size of your business and your credit history—at low rates, 6.625 percent.

"Forget about it," one Williamsburg merchant said. "You think anybody in his rightful mind would want to get back to this neighborhood?"

Forget about it?

A Harlem merchant, the owner of a clothing store on West 125th Street, said he would love to forget about it.

Looters had stolen his mannequins as well as his clothes.

"The only reason I opened up today is that I have to pay off the creditors. I want to close, but I can't afford to."

The chairman of the three-year-old Fort Greene Cooperative Supermarket, who had been anticipating the market's first year in the black and its first rebates, was surprised as much as he was angry.

The co-op's meats and produce were good, its prices competitive; it treated its customers fairly—no price hikes on payday—and with respect.

The market employed two dozen local people; it didn't even have a gate in front of its large window.

Moments after the lights went out, looters went in through that window and carted out meat, canned goods, beer, and all the cash registers.

"I thought we had deep roots in the community, but this kind of store is new to people, and I guess it will take more time."

Nearly four thousand people had been arrested.

Fewer than a third had been arraigned, and many of them remained in custody, leaving more than two thousand people in custody.

"We couldn't read the papers in court last night," said a spokesman for the Manhattan Criminal Court. "We couldn't see the faces. We had no arrest records."

The arrest records were three hours away, in Albany.

Officers raced up the thruway to retrieve them; state police met them halfway. But their best efforts were little more than a few small fingers in the dike.

A reporter asked a court officer how long it would be until all the prisoners were arraigned.

"God knows," the officer said.

The president of the Macon Street Block Association was just plain angry.

"These fools destroyed the only drugstore in the area," she said, a store owned and operated by black people. "Now we're going to have to go to the white neighborhoods to get a prescription filled."

The owner of Simon Smalls Bargain House Furniture and Appliances said he wasn't giving up.

He had bought the store, which had been on Broadway in Brooklyn for thirty-three years, eight months earlier.

Now he was out four rooms of furniture, three of them huge showrooms.

"I'm not giving up," he said. "I'm just giving up on the neighborhood."

———

"Close? How can I close?" asked the owner of the Key Food on West 116th Street, who estimated his losses, stock and damage, at $150,000.

How would I make a living? he asked.

Where would my customers shop?

I gave to all the block parties.

Supported all the community groups.

This is the way I get paid back.

The store had been there since 1919.

He planned to open the next day or the day after. Until then, his customers would have to pay three to four times his prices in the small stores.

It was the rush of customers Friday morning that spoiled the blackout for the bicycle-store manager who had so enjoyed the crickets, birds, and stars.

He called the police, but the desk sergeant told him that the precinct was too busy to do anything about looters buying parts and accessories for stolen bikes.

They took raw lumber.

They took bookcases, beds, dressers, cabinets, tables, and chairs.

They smashed empty shelves.

They ripped a radio off the radiator it had been chained to.

They left one wall untouched.

The owner of the Amsterdam Avenue store pointed to it.

It was covered with thank-you notes from children who had made things out of the wood he had donated for art and shop classes in the local schools.

"For twenty-five years I've helped all the children—black children, white children, Catholic and not Catholic, colored and not colored, and all kinds of children.

"I went through Auschwitz and Buchenwald—the only difference is that there they wore boots and here they wore sneakers."

On 138th Street in the Bronx, Ghetto Records was back open, and there was salsa music in the air.

Residents leaned out windows and gathered on fire escapes, hoping to catch a breeze.

Down on the street a small crowd wandered from one burned-out building to another, looking like tourists visiting ancient ruins.

A twenty-six-year-old unemployed salesman sipped a bottle of wine and thought about his radio.

"I worked for six months to pay one off," he said. "Broke my ass. And my son got one as soon as the lights went out. I felt like a jerk."

23

A *Daily News* columnist asked a man sitting at the counter of a doughnut shop in Bushwick if he could explain the looting.

The man owned the men's clothing store called Al-Bert's.

"The unemployment rate around here, gee, you see people window-shopping week after week, no money to buy anything, just looking, you knew something had to happen."

The owner of the doughnut shop interrupted him. "Animals," he said.

"What do you mean, animals?" asked the owner of Al-Bert's.

"It's an animal instinct I can't understand."

"How can you say that? I can't condone. But every time you have an action, there's a reaction. These people can't get jobs. They're penned in here. They reacted."

"I got a kid come in here for ice cream, a kid goes to school," the owner of the doughnut shop said. The kid wants an éclair. He reads the sign. "He says to me, 'Give me an Eclipse' . . . 'Give me an Eclipse.' You think that's right, they don't even learn to read in school?"

"Schools don't work," said the owner of Al-Bert's. "Nothing works for these people. They need jobs first."

"You're taking everything from a black viewpoint," the doughnut-shop owner said. "I went to the bank for a loan and they only asked me two things: Are you black or are you Puerto Rican? I couldn't get a loan. Hear that? Hear that?"

The columnist asked the owner of Al-Bert's to show him the store. Afterward, they went into a small cafeteria. The argument was already under way. The owner of Al-Bert's jumped right in, asking a fellow merchant how many people he thought would go and how many would stay.

"Everyone who can move and make a living elsewhere will leave. Who wouldn't?"

"Those who have some stake in the community besides money might stay," said the owner of Al-Bert's.

The man was offended.

So was the owner of the cafeteria. "What do you mean?" he asked.

"Put back something into the community."

"Put back my ass," said the cafeteria owner. "We don't do that in white neighborhoods."

"How come black doctors, when they get money, they run out of here?" the first man hollered.

"You get nowhere screaming," the cafeteria owner said. Then he screamed himself: "There's a limit. You got to do for yourself in this world."

"The limit is being without a job," said the owner of Al-Bert's.

"Jobs," the first man said. "There's all kinds of jobs."

"They got no jobs around here," the owner of Al-Bert's said. "Nothing."

The first man turned to a man who hadn't been in the conversation and said, "Tell him about the time the four of them waited for you and they—"

The owner of Al-Bert's finished the sentence: "Mugged him." He went on, "Look, I got eighteen stitches in my back, saving my mother."

"So you know," the owner of the cafeteria said.

"I didn't like it, but I understood what caused them to do it," the owner of Al-Bert's said. The way he saw it (and explained it to another reporter), people needed to "look at the total economic condition, the frame of mind of the people. . . . Window-shoppers finally got a chance to fulfill their desires and not just live with the bare necessities. Everybody stepped into the television commercial for a few hours and took what they wanted."

"You what?" the cafeteria owner asked.

"I understood."

"You understood getting mugged? You understood it? You understood it?"

24

Out on the street, the air was filled with smoke and soot, the smell of asphalt siding and burned wood, and the cries of those who had lost their homes.

It was a familiar smell.

Half the neighborhood's twelve thousand buildings were made of wood and asphalt siding, a combustible combination. One out of eight Bushwick buildings had been damaged or destroyed by fire each year since 1969.

It was not just a matter of building materials or old-law walls (those that were not fire-retardant) or old-law airshafts, which worked like chimneys when fires started below.

There were also people without jobs, uncollected trash, drinking and smoking, landlords looking to get out of a neighborhood in free fall, tenants looking to get out of horrible housing (burned-out families received special aid, and their names went up to the top of the public-housing waiting list), kids who liked to play with matches.

Three-quarters of Bushwick's fires were attributed to arson.

"In some neighborhoods kids play stickball," said an arson detective. "In Bushwick they set fires." For as little as $50, when they didn't do it for free.

On Broadway a grocer, confident the looting was over, stood in front of his store with a police baton. All Wednesday night, all day Thursday, and all Thursday night he had stood in the same spot with a shotgun.

"You have to protect yourself," he said.

"I told them . . . they were going to get hurt. They went away and robbed somebody else. Maybe tonight I'll sleep."

"I'm almost 70 years old and I have no place to go," cried a woman standing across the street from the charred remains of her $57 rental.

"I wish I had died."

"I am no bleeding heart," said the head of the Legal Aid Society's criminal-defense staff.

He'd been robbed.

He knew.

The public's rage was understandable.

Many of the suspects were creeps.

The posturing of the mayor, who had again urged prosecutors and judges to deal "forcefully" and "harshly" with the looters, was predictable.

But, the defense attorney insisted, neither rage nor posturing should mean that justice goes by the wayside.

The Manhattan DA had announced that a Class A misdemeanor was the minimum charge his office would accept for third-degree burglary. Upon conviction, that might mean a year in jail. Ordinarily, the DA's assistants would allow defendants accused of third-degree burglary to plead guilty to Class B and C misdemeanors. The most they'd serve was ninety days, and they might serve only thirty. The Queens DA had gone further: For felony burglary charges, his assistants would accept no misdemeanor pleas at all.

"A looter should not be punished more harshly than a mugger," said the defense attorney. "And suspects should not be punished at all." Justice called for reasonable—and consistent—bail and plea bargaining. But he and his colleagues feared that prosecutors, knowing many looting cases would be dropped or settled with greatly reduced charges, were trying to exact the penalty now.

The owner of Al-Bert's was back in his store, knee-deep in debris.

The shelves were empty.

Freestanding display cases had been toppled.

On the side of one hung a poster of a pensive Martin Luther King, Jr. It looked as if King were falling to the floor.

The owner had started as a stock boy and bought the store when its white owners bailed out. In no time he learned that merchants were judged not by their character but by the color of their customers' skin. Manufacturers sent him seconds and wouldn't accept returns. Banks wouldn't loan him money. His landlord refused to take any responsibility when a flood in the basement destroyed stock. He paid a security agency $400 to respond to his alarm. Burglars came; security guards didn't.

"I was looted before the blackout," he said. "The people were looted, too."

The National Shoe Store was open for business, but there was no business.

"There won't be for a long time," the manager said. "Everybody around here has new shoes."

The mayor returned to Brooklyn late Friday afternoon.

Traveling with aides, state and federal officials, and reporters in two air-conditioned buses, he hoped his second visit in twenty-four hours would make up for his absence while the power was out.

He'd been criticized.

Now he was criticized some more.

First by merchants on Broadway in Williamsburg.

"I asked the cops to stop the looting," shouted the forty-four-year-old owner of Nice and Pretty, pointing his finger at the mayor.

Stay outside and let the looters take what they want, he was told.

"They didn't stop nobody."

He had picked up a stick and started into the store.

The cops told him to put it down. You'll get hurt, they said.

Residents had the same complaint. "The people asked them to stop the looters," charged a handyman who lived on top of a furniture store that had been looted and torched, "but they didn't do nothing to them."

Even looters gave the mayor hell.

"Hey, Beame," shouted one woman, "you bum! If you want to know what to do for us, give us jobs."

"We're having a house sale," shouted a girl of about fifteen as she climbed up an accordion gate that had been ripped off a store. "We don't play now, we rob. You know what they say—when the cat's away, the mice will play."

The mayor had to go; Israeli prime minister Menachem Begin was waiting at the airport. But before he departed, he took the name of a seventy-seven-year-old woman whose house had been destroyed by fire.

She broke into tears and kissed his hand.

25

The following day, three teenagers approached a man walking alone on 104th Street near Manhattan Avenue.

"Hey, man, you want to buy a color TV or a stereo?" one of them asked, pointing toward the entryway of an abandoned building.

The television was $150. The radio, a shortwave, $25.

Anything else? the man asked.

Sure, they said: clothes, furniture, radios, and shoes.

The man asked them why they stole the stuff if they didn't need it.

"Everybody else was doing it," said the oldest of the three. He was twenty and lived with his uncle and two sisters in four rooms in a run-down building on one of the blocks between Broadway and Columbus. "If we hadn't taken the stuff, somebody else would have."

"Besides, the store owners can collect insurance."

The man pointed out that many didn't have insurance, and even those who did would not collect it right away. "What do they do now?"

"I don't know," said another of the boys, a nineteen-year-old, who said he had it better than his friends. His mother was a teacher; his father worked for the city. "I just did it for the hell of it," he said. "Maybe they will see what it's like to have nothing, and nothing to do."

"What if the stores don't reopen?" the man asked.

"Are you a cop or a preacher?" the twenty-year-old asked.

"Neither," the man said. He was a reporter.

"Look, man, we can't get no jobs here, and our families are hurting. They can take it and we can't."

"How is looting going to help?" the reporter asked the third boy, who was seventeen and lived with his mother and five siblings in an apartment he said he was ashamed to take friends to. His mother made a little money as a spiritual adviser. His older sisters worked, but he didn't know what they did. The family was on welfare.

He said he didn't know. "I took some clothes because that's what my family needed, but none of the ones I took fit any of us and my mother told me to get them out of the house. So now I have to try to sell them to somebody."

A middle-aged woman approached on the sidewalk, frowned, and then veered off into the street.

"What's wrong?" the nineteen-year-old asked her.

"You know what's wrong," she said. "Taking something that don't belong to you is wrong."

The boys laughed.

"It won't be so funny when you land in jail and your parents can't get you out."

"Ah, go ahead on, lady, you don't know what you are talking about," the youngest said.

A young woman joined the group. "The rich get away with all their crimes. They didn't do nothing to that man that robbed all those old folks in his old folks' home," she said, referring to the nursing-home scandal uncovered in 1974. Owners and operators stole millions of Medicaid dollars, paid off public officials, and abused the elderly and indigent in their care.

"They never do nothing if you are rich or a politician. Some of them stores deserved to be ripped off because they cheat us all the time, charging high prices for junk."

"Lord help us," the older woman said.

"Lord help us," one of the boys said.

Then they fled. One of them had spotted a police car. They returned for their merchandise the moment the car was out of sight.

26

Merchants were furious. Furious at the looters. Furious at the police. Furious at their insurance companies. Furious at the mayor.

But few knew who had looted their stores.

Insurance agents were impossible to reach.

And only the very brave, or foolish, were inclined to speak their minds to the police.

That left the mayor.

Everywhere he went, merchants complained about the police. The mayor defended them. They did everything they could do, he said.

Everything but shoot, even though in some places, snipers shot at them. One officer was shot in the leg. Four hundred eighteen were injured, eighteen seriously. Unlike 1968, when officers simply cordoned off areas (and none were hurt seriously), they went into crowds and made arrests, nearly four thousand.

They couldn't arrest everyone. They were badly outnumbered.

The police commissioner put it plainly: "If each officer were to go out and grab the first person he saw, it would have meant that very shortly there would have been no cops on the street at all."

"We fought for years to preserve this area," said the owner of a Flatbush Avenue hearing-aid business.

As past president of the chamber of commerce and a current

member of the planning board, he had begged fellow business-men not to move to Kings Plaza.

"And here I get a call at two a.m. telling me there's looting, and my building's burning.

"Why wasn't the Guard called out?" he asked.

The worst of the looting was over long before Guardsmen could have been mustered, the mayor said.

"Thirty years of my life have gone down the drain," the man said. "And of course every store owner who can possibly leave is leaving. We need more personal responsibility."

And we needed the National Guard.

The merchants whom the mayor met in the Bronx were less interested in what had happened than what would happen now.

"What about the people who are unemployed as a result of the riots?" asked the manager of a men's clothing store destroyed by fire. On his block of St. Ann's Avenue alone, near the corner of 138th Street, two dozen people were out of jobs.

"I have to pay my rent, I've got a family, a car, a house, a mortgage, and bank loans. What am I going to do?"

Businesses will reopen, the mayor promised.

There will be small grants. Large loans.

You will have your jobs back.

Soon.

"Is this a riot?" asked one of the owners of Alec Zander, the Bronx furniture store, at a meeting at Sutter's Bakery.

"The Small Business Administration has already declared the city a disaster area," the mayor said. That would mean low-interest loans. Next week, he added, the governor would apply for federal disaster relief.

Is a disaster the same as a riot?

Next week, the mayor repeated, the governor would apply to

the federal government for disaster status. If granted, it would mean grants and additional low-interest loans.

"Forgive my rudeness," the man said, "but you're not answering my question." He reminded the mayor that he'd had hundreds of people in his store. "That's a riot."

"It was not a riot," the mayor said.

"How do we get insured? How do we stay?"

"Oh, come on," the mayor said. "Don't say you haven't heard. You're pushing aside what I'm telling you."

"Is this different from Watts? Is this different from Newark?"

The Bronx DA stepped forward. It didn't matter what the mayor called it, he said. Merchants would need lawyers to negotiate with their insurance companies.

"I ask a question," said the owner of the furniture store, "I get a political answer."

Back at City Hall, the mayor called a news conference to announce a city-sponsored emergency relief fund. He called on labor, business, and banking leaders to contribute. The fund would provide cash grants to merchants, money they could get immediately and would not have to pay back.

Reporters asked several questions about backlogs in the courts and reports of severe overcrowding and atrocious conditions in detention pens and city jails.

The mayor brushed them aside. He didn't want to hear about the looters.

It was their victims who needed help.

We need, he said, to "get money into the hands of these people immediately."

27

The editors of *The New York Times* had rushed to print with an editorial that offered an explanation of the looting. Their readers read it and rushed to their typewriters, summoned their secretaries, armed themselves with paper, pens, pencils, envelopes, and stamps.

"You still try to justify their behavior," one Manhattan man wrote to the editor. "They live on welfare and rip off the Federal Government on all the anti-poverty programs. We either cut them off completely, or we will have to face a drastic evaluation of the situation. The Puerto Ricans can go back to P.R. They belong there anyway and if the blacks do not shape up they can go back to the South.

"The warning should have gone out that every looter would be shot on the spot."

"I am shocked and stunned and aghast," wrote another, "to read you think that since the rules of society do not work for these people, they do not have to play by the rules."

No group has received more time, attention, or money.

"They give nothing and expect everything as their right."

I am "tired of reading the same 1930s explanation about why the poor do what they do. It sounds like an undergraduate sociology text that badly needs revision.

"I have never known anyone who came from the poor and met

with success in life who was not responsible for his behavior and didn't know the rules of the game."

Hundreds of people wrote letters.

The editors published dozens of them, but not before they responded to the first wave.

They acknowledged the force of first impressions—the smoke, the glass, the litter, the "anguished" faces of the looted merchants, "the lithe, dark, young bodies" of the looters, the blows to civility, struggling neighborhoods, and the city's economy and reputation—as well as the force of emotions that those impressions gave rise to.

But there was more to understanding than first impressions.

"Profound problems of race and poverty still lurk just beneath the surface of this fruitful society."

"Excuses," wrote one of the paper's own columnists.

The looting had nothing to do with race or poverty.

Looters looted indiscriminately. Although black and Hispanic New Yorkers were unfortunately lumped together with them, they were the looters' worst victims. And they were among those calling the looters animals. "In a non-racial sense they were right": The looters were without human guilt.

Nor was the looting a matter of poverty. Poverty was greater when the lights went out in 1965, the standard of living lower. Looters stole "toasters, not bread," "liquor, not milk."

Why? Because they believed that "stealing is okay, if you can get away with it." If the opportunity arises, you go for it. Anyone who doesn't is a loser or a jerk.

That "non-ethic" followed naturally from the idea that welfare was a right as opposed to a last resort; that past wrongs entitled minority reparations; that crime was the result of poverty, and poverty the fault of the system; and that society owed you not just freedom and opportunity, but "the good life."

The prominence of a few members of a few minority groups has "masked the enduring torments of poverty and race," wrote the editors.

"Bushwick, Brownsville, East Harlem and Williamsburg" are "miles beyond the ken of the thriving and thrusting Americans who make policy and mold opinions." The people who live there are less visible than ever. Their invisibility "makes their situation more hopeless, and they know it." They are "victims of economic and social forces (the decline of manufacturing, the loss of jobs to the suburbs and the Third World) that they sense but do not understand."

The editors deplored the violence and the losses.

They expected police and prosecutors would punish as many criminals as possible.

But some of the city's troubles were self-inflicted.

"We did not spend enough of our ingenuity and our affluence to solve the problems the riots of the 60s made evident."

"If only we had heeded the lessons of the 1960s and spent more money, you say," wrote a Long Island man.

But he thought that most people had learned a very different lesson from the 1960s: "The great majority of the publicly funded programs then begun were utter fiascos." They did nothing for the poor. Instead, "they enriched poverty-program bureaucrats." Meanwhile, crime increased. "Once-stable neighborhoods" were "destroyed. . . . Schools became jungles. Businesses left in disgust and the middle class fled in despair.

"Let us stop analyzing the problems of the wolves while they are slaughtering the sheep. Rather let us treat the wolves more like wolves while there are still more of us sheep."

"Of course society must protect itself," the editors replied.

"Of course the police must maintain order and criminals must be punished swiftly and certainly."

But if that's all we learn from the looting, we are in trouble.

If the looters are wolves or any other kind of animal, we need to "heed" them.

"In the blindness of that night, New York and America could see rage."

"Rage?" asked a reader from Roslyn Heights. "If the television coverage of the blackout looting is to be believed, 'rage' was hardly the prevailing emotion.

"Glee more accurately describes what we saw and it is in no one's interest to characterize it in nobler terms."

Sure there was glee on Wednesday night, or at least abandon, admitted a professor of Africana studies who took to the op-ed pages like a professional wrestler whose tag-team partner was getting clobbered. Sentiment was running against the editors, twenty to one.

But, the professor insisted, anyone who walked the streets earlier that day, or the day before, would be struck not by glee but by desperation, "desperation that has too many strong, healthy people sitting around for months at a time, waiting for jobs that will never materialize, looking for chances America now admits it cannot provide.

"The welfare agencies may buy what people need, but in a nation of such conspicuous consumption . . . such measures are just not adequate.

"People steal, or loot, or riot, because they do not have the money to buy what they want." New York's poor live "within whistling distance of the richest people in the country." How can you tell them that there are things that they can't have "because they have dark skin?"

"Bah!" wrote a reader from Far Rockaway.
"Looters are born, not made."

28

The criminal courts in four boroughs had doubled the number of judges and lengthened bench shifts. Some judges were working around the clock.

The Legal Aid Society added lawyers.

The district attorney's office added prosecutors.

Yet Sunday morning there were still more than fourteen hundred prisoners awaiting arraignment. And, whether it was because judges would not set bail until rap sheets arrived from Albany, or because defendants could not possibly post the bail they had set, many of those who had been arraigned remained in jail.

Court officials blamed the police.

To arraign a defendant, they needed, in addition to the defendant, a formal complaint, sworn statements, the defendant's criminal record, and a police officer, preferably the arresting officer.

It was up to arresting officers to put the pieces together, and they had failed to do so.

Court officials had heard every excuse: Officers were home resting after working around the clock; or they were at a hospital nursing wounds; or they were back on the streets (the mayor had ordered beefed-up patrols, fifteen hundred extra officers, on Friday and Saturday).

But no matter where they had been, no matter where they were now, DAs couldn't arraign without them.

Defense attorneys insisted that even if the police were wholly responsible for the backlog in arraignments, they couldn't be blamed for the excessive charges that prosecutors were pressing—or the number of people who remained in jail even though they had been arraigned. No. It was the DAs and judges who, with the encouragement of the mayor, had abandoned the city's usual guidelines for plea bargaining and bail.

Lawyers for the ACLU and Legal Aid complained bitterly about blackout bail.

Men with families, arrested for the first time, were usually released on their own recognizance, an ACLU lawyer told a reporter. Now those same men, charged with looting, were being asked to post $1,000, at the very least. "Most bails are running $2,500 if the person has no record and $5,000 with a record," the lawyer said. "Those charged with burglary first offense are getting $2,500, which is way out of line. . . . Bail is being used for punitive reasons. It is my impression that very few people are getting out."

The head of the Legal Aid Society's criminal defense staff said he had no objection to $1,000 bail for a looter with a lengthy criminal record who was carrying a loaded .38 without a permit. But $10,000 for a suspect with no criminal record accused of "exiting through a broken window" with nothing in his hands? That's "nonsense."

Prosecutors blamed Legal Aid attorneys for slowing things down; for example, they had so far refused to waive the full reading of rights and charges in the courtroom, thereby extending the time of every arraignment from a few minutes to at least fifteen or twenty.

It was a deliberate slowdown, some said, a protest against the treatment of prisoners in the detention cells and in the court-room.

Some Legal Aid attorneys acknowledged that it was, but their boss denied it, and one weary Manhattan judge simply could not believe that defense attorneys would protest their clients' incarceration in that way.

"If you've got time, I've got time," he said, "but your client is not in the most comfortable of conditions, and you're just keeping him there."

29

On Sunday, three days after the blackout, Con Edison's president walked reporters around the Control Center. At one point, he stood alongside a console of switches and buttons just to the left of the system operator's chair. It was a manual load-shedding console, installed shortly after the blackout of 1965, and it controlled a quarter of the city's electricity.

The last line to the north was lost at 9:20 p.m. Wednesday evening, the president explained. At 9:36, the system shut down. The system operator had about fifteen minutes to throw some or all of those load-shedding switches. Hundreds of thousands of customers, maybe more, would have been without power. But restoration would have been simpler and much quicker. And by intentionally shedding load, he might have saved the system.

It was a matter of judgment, the president said. The operator was working with a theoretical generating capacity of nearly 10 million kilowatts from plants that Con Edison owned in whole or in part. That evening he was supplying just under 6 million kilowatts of electricity, half of which was imported because it was cheaper to buy than to generate. The system adjusted to the initial loss of power so quickly that it barely registered on the operator's display. Thus, despite the loss to lightning of four or five lines in Westchester, and later the imminent loss of Con Edison's ties to Long Island and New Jersey, the system operator and his dispatcher apparently believed—and had reason to believe—that they could keep the system running without shedding load.

Once engineers studied the logs and computer printouts from that evening, they would have a better idea of exactly what had happened and why. But the president said he had already approved a series of measures intended to strengthen the system. Those measures included the overhaul of the ignitions of the city's older gas turbines, which would allow operators to start them more quickly; the staffing of those turbines around the clock; and the installation of backup generators at substations in order to provide emergency power and light.

30

First thing Monday morning, city officials and the city's congressional delegation met with President Carter's counsel to talk about disaster relief.

It didn't go well.

The president's counsel said that the blackout and blackout looting were not natural disasters, not acts of God, and therefore not the kinds of disasters for which Congress meant to provide relief. A final decision would follow the governor's formal application, but he thought it unlikely that the city would be declared a disaster area.

The Small Business Administration announced that on Monday it would open six special offices, two in northern Manhattan and one in each of the outer boroughs, to process applications for loans.

Merchants began to gather at sunrise. Even in Staten Island, where there had been little looting, dozens of people turned up, most of them with stores in Manhattan and Brooklyn. They had traveled across the Narrows hoping to avoid long lines.

Lines formed and lines grew. The offices were not scheduled to open until two p.m.

Firemen in Bushwick didn't need the White House or the SBA to know which way the neighborhood was going; it was as much of a disaster on Monday as it had been on the day of the blackout. In the early afternoon they were called to an abandoned knitting factory on the corner of Myrtle and Knickerbocker. Witnesses had seen a small group of men they knew to be drug addicts leaving the building. Soon after, they saw smoke.

Heat and lightning are certainly acts of God, said members of the city's congressional delegation, speaking to reporters after they left the meeting with the president's counsel.

And both had contributed to the blackout.

Interpreted narrowly, the statute would unfairly slight the cities.

New York was hit as hard by the blackout as Gulf fishermen by the cold winter or Iowa farmers by the drought.

The lines outside the SBA offices continued to grow, prompting officials to open their doors two hours early. But staffs were small and applications several pages long. The lines moved slowly.

Some complained bitterly about the delays: first Con Edison, then the city, now the feds. "No one," one man said, "is making it easy for us."

Most thought half a day's hassles a small price to pay for the possibility of a large low-interest loan.

It was a ten-alarm blaze at the knitting factory, which meant that every fire company in Brooklyn and many in Manhattan answered the call—fifty-five units, three hundred firemen in all.

By a coincidence of shifts, many of those firemen had spent the day of the blackout in Bushwick.

It had been 92 degrees that day. It was now 98.

The heat from the fire melted the windows of several fire trucks.

Collapsing brick buildings buried a dozen cars.

The mayor remained hopeful about federal aid.

He hadn't expected disaster status.

He had spoken to the president, who was sympathetic. They planned to meet the following day. There were other sources of money in Washington, and here at home, business and labor leaders had endorsed the mayor's proposal for a rescue fund, three and a half million dollars, available immediately.

"Now they know how it feels to be poor," said the director of the El Barrio Chamber of Commerce, standing near a line of merchants waiting to apply for a loan.

Some of those merchants lived miles from East Harlem.

That bothered him.

"Now they know how it feels to apply to the government for money, the way welfare clients have to," he said. "If they had shown some interest in the community, they might not have been looted."

The president said nothing about disaster relief.

Six months into his presidency, Jimmy Carter's short honeymoon was long over. Congress had buried his farm program and put his plans for tax cuts, tax reform, and welfare reform on hold.

He was thinking about energy.

The blackout, he said, was proof—if oil embargoes and gas lines were not proof enough—of the need for a national energy policy, a coordinated effort to use less, produce more, and develop alternatives to coal and oil. If we succeeded, we would dramatically reduce our dependence on imports. It was the moral equivalent of war.

He asked his Cabinet for a report on the feasibility of a national power grid. He asked his defense secretary for a report on readiness of the National Guard. And he asked the Federal Power Commission for a report on the causes of the blackout. He wanted the FPC report in ten days.

31

On Tuesday, Con Edison's chairman told a New York State board of inquiry that despite the system operator's decision not to shed load manually, the network's automatic load-shedding system—an elaborate array of relays and circuit breakers also installed after the blackout of 1965—should have prevented the recent outage.

It was too soon to know for sure why it didn't.

But engineers had a hypothesis.

Until very late in the crisis, the utility drew a steady supply of power from New Jersey and Long Island, thereby maintaining its normal current frequency of sixty cycles. The load-shedding relays also registered a normal current frequency of sixty cycles and therefore did not shed any load. When the system lost those last two ties, it shut down.

32

Lawyers for the Emergency Committee for Prisoners' Release filed suit against the city in federal court.

They spoke of beatings, of prisoners who weren't allowed to make phone calls, of rats in detention pens, of rotten food and hot soup in 100-degree heat, of overflowing toilets, of heroin addicts without methadone, and of epileptics, diabetics, and pregnant women without medical care.

The law said that if a suspect was not granted a hearing within seventy-two hours of his arrest, the court had to show cause for the delay or release him. If it didn't, the suspect could seek dismissal of charges for the delay alone.

The blackout suspects had now been incarcerated for five days.

The committee wanted $500 million in damages, and it wanted the judge to order the mayor, police commissioner, corrections commissioner, and administrative judge of the criminal courts to show cause why all the remaining suspects should not be freed.

"We are sick and tired of hearing you always supporting the lawbreakers," one New Yorker wrote to the Legal Aid Society. "If they don't like jail conditions, let them obey the law. Have you expressed any sympathy for the storekeepers whose lifetime work was wiped out in a night of looting? That would be too much to ask of you bleeding hearts."

Scores of people wrote angry letters to Legal Aid, and so many people telephoned that the switchboard operator stopped putting outside calls through.

The director tried to explain. Legal Aid would most certainly represent needy merchants in bankruptcy pleadings and loan closings. As for the defense of people arrested for looting, the lawsuits intended to speed up their arraignments, and the monitoring of prison conditions—that was Legal Aid's job, a job it did with federal funds since the Supreme Court, in *Gideon*, held that states must provide counsel for poor people accused of crimes.

"Why Legal Aid should get all this flak for defending people is beyond me," the director said. "We are doing our best to carry out our responsibility and uphold our laws, unpopular though it may be at this moment. This is the only way to guarantee a just and civilized society."

33

With the mercury above 100 all week, Con Edison executives would have liked to spend less time trying to explain the blackout and more time trying to prevent another one. But reporters, public officials, and regulators wanted an explanation. They didn't get one; they got lots of them.

First, and for days, executives said it was lightning. Then on Sunday Con Edison's president hinted that the system operator might have erred when he decided not to shed load. On Tuesday morning the chairman told the state board of inquiry that the system's automatic load-shedding devices failed to shed load, a failure which led directly to the outage.

But just a few hours later, Con Edison's president told *The New York Times*'s top technology reporter that the automatic load-shedding devices had shed too much load too quickly.

Moments before the system shut down, the president explained, the load on Con Edison's tie to New Jersey greatly exceeded its capacity. To save itself, New Jersey opened the line. Thousands of load-shedding relays, registering the loss and the ensuing gap between generation and demand, began to cut power to hundreds of thousands of customers. But the sudden, dramatic load-shedding created imbalances, "surpluses as dangerous as deficits," and the surpluses overloaded two local generators, creating a deficit that the generators remaining on line could not make up.

In other words, the president said, it wasn't that automatic load shedding did not work. It worked too well.

34

The Emergency Committee had asked for the immediate release of all the blackout prisoners who had yet to be arraigned.

Too late, the city's lawyers responded in court the following day. All the blackout prisoners had been arraigned.

What's more, said the deputy mayor for criminal justice (well aware how unpalatable the news he was about to report would be), three out of four of them were already back on the street.

Some—including many without criminal records—pleaded guilty to minor charges and were freed on time served.

Some, released without bail, would face trial later.

And some posted bail, awaiting trial or consideration of their cases by a grand jury.

There were, to be sure, prisoners awaiting arraignment in the city's courts. Hundreds, all of them arrested after the blackout.

Nonetheless, if the committee agreed to drop its suit, the city would work with it to ensure that not a single blackout prisoner was lost in the system.

Neither the city's lawyers nor the deputy major said anything about conditions in the prisons.

But the mayor did.

"Bleeding-heart stories," he said. "I have no sympathy for the looters stuck in jail."

Five of the prisoners awaiting arraignment had been arrested earlier that morning after police in the 24th Precinct, acting on a tip from a neighbor, stormed an apartment on West 108th Street in Manhattan and found themselves in the middle of a narcotics factory and fencing warehouse.

They grabbed four men and a woman.

Three others jumped from a window, twenty feet to the sidewalk, when the police came in.

It took ten officers three hours to load three rooms of clothes, car radios and tape decks, televisions, portable stereos, bicycles, cameras, auto supplies, small appliances, triple-beam balances, two ounces of cocaine, many pounds of marijuana, $6,000 in small bills, a loaded shotgun, and four pistols into police vans and transport it to the station.

Later, the mayor and police visited the precinct house to congratulate the detectives.

It was $100,000 worth of contraband, the commissioner said, the largest recovery of blackout loot to date.

But officers interviewed afterward said that whatever its value, it wasn't all blackout loot.

"It's possible that some of the brand-new items were stolen during the blackout," one detective said. "But a lot of the stuff was secondhand, typical of a swap-shop operation for stolen property, which is traded for drugs or cash."

And some of the new stuff—dresses with Macy's tags, for example—was definitely not stolen that night.

35

The lights had been back on for a week.

The blackout prisoners had all been arraigned.

Sales of flashlights, batteries, portable radios, candles, smoke detectors, canned food, and bottled water had dropped off precipitously, sorely disappointing merchants who had doubled and tripled their orders in anticipation of a great late July.

The debate about the looting still raged.

"Sin began with Adam," said the U.S. ambassador to the United Nations, who had been in Switzerland during the blackout. "All men sin and fall short of the glory of God. If you turn the lights out some will steal. They will do that in Switzerland, too.

"But, more seriously," he added, "they will do that especially if they are hungry. And you've got to realize that in New York you are probably running at unemployment levels of about 30 to 40 percent among young adults."

Does the ambassador "mean to imply that the huge dude running down the street with a 150-pound sofa hoisted over his head was suffering from malnutrition?" asked a syndicated columnist. And that "those cats who looted the auto dealer in the Bronx, driving 50 shiny new Pontiacs right through the showroom window," did it because "they had been denied three square meals a day? . . . If hunger was in back of it all," he asked, "how come some of the welfare mommas filmed ripping off jewelry, clothing, and liquor stores lumbered about like overfed heifers who could use six months on a liquid protein diet?"

The ambassador was an "ideologue," the columnist wrote, speaking "sociological drivel—futile attempts to mitigate responsibility for savage behavior by appeals to the alleged poverty and joblessness of those involved."

New York City had taxed and spent itself into bankruptcy aiding the poor: "Hundreds of billions of dollars" for welfare, food stamps, housing allowances, unemployment relief, social security, educational aid and legal aid, Medicare and Medicaid. The idea was that we could buy "a happier, safer, saner society," a "great society."

That idea was a "fraud."

The "burned-out buildings" were the "perfect metaphor" for the ruins of the liberal philosophy that had guided the city.

The cause of the latest "barbarism" was not parsimony but permissiveness, not a lack of jobs—let alone food—but the absence of the "moral fiber" and "values" that "family and church provide."

Unemployment, the president told a correspondent for the National Black Network, was the "number one" cause of the looting.

There is no excuse for the violence, he went on. "But it is also important that public officials like myself try to understand the reasons for it. . . . Obviously the number one contributing factor to crime of all kinds is high unemployment among young people, particularly those who are black or Spanish-speaking" and have "such a difficult time getting jobs" in hard times.

He promised a "flood of new programs" in the coming weeks, programs made possible by money recently appropriated for jobs, housing, and food stamps.

Welfare reform alone, he said, would bring one million new jobs.

The editors of *The New Republic* agreed that the unemployed needed jobs, real jobs, productive jobs.

But they doubted that a jobs program was on its way.

There had been no "clamor," they wrote, "to revive the war on poverty." And that wasn't simply because, since 1975, when a big bond sale failed and the city's fiscal crisis became apparent, there had been so little money to go around.

Rather, people had come to agree that money could not solve New York's problems. If it could, the city wouldn't have any. No city had been more generous. Countless lives may have been improved, but the looting showed the poor to be "more desperate and dangerous than before."

What's more, unlike the riots of the 1960s, the looting was not a protest against racism, segregation, ghetto life, or the murder of Martin Luther King, Jr.

It was a mugging, in a mugger's city. "How do you rally around the mugger's cause?"

Government could and should help with jobs, but jobs were not all that the poorest black people needed. They also needed "cohesive values and personal ambition," and those were "not gifts which the white majority" could "bestow." Black leaders, inclined mostly to speak words of defiance to whites, must also speak to and work with fellow blacks.

The "sociological explanation" would not do. At best (those rare instances when it was not "intended and taken as justification"), it was "much too facile, indiscriminate, and debilitating."

The author of a "Talk of the Town" piece in *The New Yorker* thought that the sociological explanation had much to recommend it. He also thought that the attitude of all those who so cavalierly dismissed it was "set so defiantly against the facts" that it suggested just one conclusion: "The attitude toward the riots caused the riots."

Throughout history, he wrote, poverty had created crime: "People without jobs, and without any hope of getting jobs, are likely to steal. They always have been and they always will be. And when people not only are helplessly poor but are excluded from ordinary society—as the great majority of non-whites are from this white society—they have little reason to live by that society's moral traditions or obey that society's laws."

36

The chairman of the Board of Correction concluded that the delays in the courtrooms and conditions in the prisons added up to "a denial of constitutional safeguards" and a failure to dispense "rational human justice."

Ten days after the blackout, he held hearings to try to determine what went wrong.

The most spectacular witness was a twenty-six-year-old man who testified that he had been held for six days without access to a phone, lawyer, or judge, in "unbearably hot" and crowded cells, first in the 42nd Precinct and then in the Bronx House of Detention.

The water wasn't drinkable, and the hamburgers were so rotten "you could smell the stink even though they burned it. . . . We slept on the floor with our hands next to our body like the slaves brought over from Africa.

"We were just by ourselves. Nobody out there was for us except our families."

Boys packed in with men and not protected from them.

It was "an American nightmare.

"This can't be true," he said to himself. "This is New York City. This is supposed to be the center of the world."

The deputy mayor for criminal justice read a statement in which he defended both the police and the justice system as a whole.

The chairman of the board rose.

Defense attorneys and civil libertarians had charged that the mayor and district attorneys had made a conscious decision, a political decision, to sacrifice due process, to appear tough on crime. The chair asked the deputy mayor if that was true.

No, said the deputy mayor. There was no decision to sacrifice due process. But there was a conscious decision to keep as many police officers as possible out on the streets.

In the end, no one was killed.

No one was seriously injured.

The Department of Correction, without advance notice, processed thousands of detainees. The system "staggered," but it did not break down.

The mayor did not attend the hearings.

But he sent a letter to the chair.

It was an extraordinary emergency, he wrote. Keeping the peace and enforcing the law called for extraordinary measures. During and after the blackout, "large numbers of people faced hardships," including the detainees. The city had to decide whether to "overload its prisons" or "overload its morgues."

"It chose the prisons."

37

A labor historian, writing on the op-ed page of *The New York Times*, called all the talk of "animals" "sadly predictable."

That, he said, was how the rich and powerful always talked about the poor and powerless. When Irish railroad workers in Jersey City sought wages owed to them, New Jersey newspaper editors called them animals. Chicago editors referred to the city's immigrant poor as "Bohemian beasts" and "Slavonic wolves." And when, in 1902, a group of Jewish women, most of them Orthodox and living in poverty on the Lower East Side, staged a dramatic protest against the rising price of kosher beef, editors called them "dangerous," "ignorant," without "inbred or acquired respect for law," "a pack of wolves."

Retail kosher butchers had promised the women that they would boycott price-gouging wholesalers. When they didn't, the women battered the butchers' shops and threw their meat into the streets. The riot spread to Brownsville, East Harlem, Williamsburg, the South Bronx, and Newark, and though the protestors paused for the Sabbath, the riot went on for days. Dozens of women were beaten by police and thrown in jail.

The animal metaphors, the historian wrote, separate "the behavior of the discontented poor (striking, rioting, looting, boycotting) from the conditions that shape their discontent." They distance the powerful from the powerless, and they "prevent us from understanding what 'they' are telling 'us' about themselves and their condition," prevent us from comprehending "the pained message that came to us on the deplorably misnamed 'night of the animals.' "

The historian, of all people, "should know the difference between protesters and looters," wrote a New Jersey man, in a letter to the editor.

So many readers were offended by the historian's analogy that the editors printed three full columns of letters and gave the historian another column to defend himself. "Readers who objected to my comparison," he explained, "missed my main point."

The historian should know the difference between a "reflexive reaction to an unpredictable emergency" and a "premeditated, organized civil disobedience, pursuant to American tradition," wrote a New York City man.

The events were different, the historian replied. But "the use of animal metaphors" by the "well-to-do" was "the same."

The kosher meat rioters were moved by "a sense of moral and religious outrage," wrote a New York woman. The looters were "merely making the most of an advantageous situation." The "lack of an internalized code of morality" made the animal metaphor apt.

The historian insisted that he had compared the reactions to the two events, not the events themselves. "History teaches us that a thin line connects the orderly and the disorderly. But the animal metaphor transmutes that thin line into a space—a crevice"—that separates "us" from "them."

"The fact that these two groups were denounced in similar terms . . . does not prove that their actions, attitudes or motives were similar," wrote a Massachusetts man. He noted that the historian himself had acknowledged that the rioting women had a "clear objective." And a "moral focus."

The events were different, yet the powerful responded the same way. They called the powerless animals. "Animal metaphors," the historian argued, "have been almost universally applied to the lower classes of society."

Not so, wrote the Massachusetts man. The use of animal metaphors was "common to all efforts to dehumanize." In recent history, the police and other figures of power and authority had been called pigs. And during and after the blackout, another reader wrote, it was not "the successful and powerful who used animal metaphors to distance themselves from the behavior of the poor." It was the people closest to them, residents and merchants of the looted neighborhoods, the poor but "law-abiding citizens who were understandably repulsed by the behavior of those who displayed a complete lack of moral standards and regard for the rights of others."

The analogy was not meant to condone looting, or to encourage it.

The Jewish women had "a real grievance," wrote a New York man. "They expressed themselves by direct action only against the retailers whom they felt were the cause of their misery." They destroyed "overpriced meat," but they didn't "steal," "wantonly destroy property," "attack anyone not directly involved," or "loot. . . . Despite their poverty, they were intelligent, educated, and had basic respect for law and order."

Yes, they had a real grievance. Yes, they had respect for law and order. But why, then, did the newspapers describe them as "a pack of wolves"? Why were they "so completely misper-ceived"?

The historian had done "a great disservice" to our grand-mothers and grandfathers and all those "who put their bodies on the line to right social wrongs," wrote a New York woman. "How can he mention in the same breath, let alone draw implicit com-parisons between, those brave souls who risked life and limb to speak out against greed and the looters who sought only selfish gain?"

"The events differed," the historian acknowledged. "So did the societies in which they occurred." The immigrant poor faced many difficulties. But there were many more jobs than workers, jobs even for people without education or skills. Think about how much harder immigrant life would have been if half the young immigrants could not get jobs.

It was now "a cliché among social scientists that poverty per se does not lead to antisocial behavior," concluded the Massa-chusetts man. "Internalized moral restraints" and "family struc-ture" were at least as important, and we ought to be able to talk about them without talking about animals. Police repression would not stop looting, but neither would a view that "absolves the looters of any responsibility on account of their poverty and implies that the application of moral criteria to their behavior is misplaced."

38

"Under any reasonable definition, the blackout was a catas-
trophe," New York's governor wrote to the president.

Despite White House hints that federal disaster status was
unlikely, the governor and the city's congressional delegation
continued to press for it.

The word "natural" did not appear in the Disaster Relief and
Emergency Assistance Act, they noted. The Act didn't distin-
guish between natural and man-made disasters.

The White House was still considering New York's request
when, on July 23, the labor secretary traveled to New York and,
with the mayor at his side, announced an $11.3 million aid
package.

The mayor was delighted. The package included money for
demolition, community redevelopment, and jobs. It didn't pre-
clude either disaster status or other sources of federal aid.

Standing behind the mayor and the labor secretary were
members of New York's congressional delegation, two of whom,
Herman Badillo and Edward Koch, were challenging the mayor
for the Democratic Party mayoral nomination.

They were not as pleased as he was.

During the news conference, they sighed and mumbled.

Afterward, Badillo, who represented the South Bronx, tore
into the package.

"We have 12,000 abandoned buildings; the aid package will

allow us to demolish 120 of them. We have hundreds of thousands looking for work; the aid package will create jobs for 2,000." Among those two thousand, he said, would undoubtedly be some looters. In other words, the government would pay criminals "to clean up the mess they made." The program was a "sop" and a "fraud," "a cover-up for federal inaction. They should really declare the city a disaster area."

"Carter said he would never tell New York City to drop dead," said Koch, who represented New York's 18th congressional district (the "silk stocking district," his opponents loved to say, especially when they campaigned in the outer boroughs). He was referring to the *New York Post* headline—FORD TO CITY: DROP DEAD—the day after the president's predecessor announced his opposition to federal loan guarantees for the financially prostrate city.

"In fact," Koch said, "Carter just did."

The mayor should never have praised the aid package.

39

Con Edison had promised three reports on the blackout.

The last week of July, it delivered the first. Little of it was new, but close readers did note that engineers had concluded there were only two lightning strikes, two or three fewer than they initially thought. The first came at 8:37, the second eighteen minutes later. Each knocked out two lines, only one of which was immediately restored. Engineers had yet to determine why two other lines—both of them critical feeders running between Pleasant Valley and Millwood—had opened up, cutting off the utility's last tie to the north.

Con Ed's president traced the chain of events from the first lightning strike to the blackout, but he offered no comprehensive explanation. Engineers, he said, were still analyzing the data. What was clear was that the system was fundamentally sound. The best proof was the utility's performance the week after the blackout, when the temperature reached 104 degrees and the demand for electricity was higher than it had ever been before.

40

Whether because they couldn't afford it or couldn't get it, many merchants had no insurance. But even those who had it didn't know if they were going to be able to collect.

"Our policy covers damage by riots, but the mayor hasn't declared this a riot," said a South Bronx merchant, standing in the showroom of his East Tremont Avenue furniture store.

He and his partner couldn't get theft insurance on East Tremont. But their fire insurance had a riot rider. They'd lost $100,000 of merchandise, and like so many other merchants, they anxiously awaited the outcome of ongoing negotiations between insurance-company executives and government regulators.

The owner of a nearby liquor store was not optimistic.

He had $20,000 of fire insurance and $40,000 worth of losses.

An adjuster had already been by.

The looting, the adjuster said, was not a riot.

"The ACLU is very concerned about the looters and their treatment in jail," said the owner of the liquor store. But, he added bitterly, there was very little assistance for the victims of crime.

In an interview on Friday, July 29, the president let slip that the White House had decided to deny the city federal disaster status.

The blackout, he said, was not a disaster under federal law.

The president's aides, who had hoped to inform the mayor and governor before they made an official announcement, rushed out of the room. There was still time to call them before they heard it on the news.

On the phone, they emphasized a point the president had made only in passing: The administration had already come up with all the money it could. The decision was less legal than political and economic. Disaster status would have meant that the city was eligible for an additional $12 million, to cover the cost of overtime for policemen and firefighters. That money simply was not available.

The mayor expressed disappointment in the president but remained upbeat: There were other avenues of federal aid to explore, and he was exploring them.

The SBA had made available $100 million.

And the city's Emergency Aid Committee was within $700,000 of its goal. The mayor urged reporters to spread the word, so that everyone eligible would apply.

The owner of Merchants couldn't even get an adjuster to come by.

"If you have a fire, you are deluged with adjusters who call you at all hours of the day and night," he said. "They want your business, ten percent of what you collect.

"Nobody called. I didn't get one call."

He called his insurance agent, told him what had happened. "What are we going to do?" he asked.

"Nothing," the agent said. "You don't have burglary insurance."

"What do you mean burglary? It was a riot."

"No, it was burglary."

"What is the definition of a riot, violence by three or more people assembled for common purpose?"

"No, no, no," the agent said.

Skeptics had mocked the mayor's Emergency Aid Committee. Even if it met its goal of $3.5 million, they said, each merchant would receive only a few thousand.

The mayor had pressed ahead. The city contributed $1 million. Business and labor put up the rest.

Twelve hundred individuals also pitched in.

A Brooklyn woman, embarrassed by the looting and terribly sorry for its victims, sent her social security increase.

A merchant sent a small check to help other small merchants, whose plight he could understand. A Hispanic man himself, he wanted people to know that whatever it looked like in the newspaper photographs or on the news, only a fraction of any community had looted. "For the most part," he said, "our people acted in a commendatory manner."

A Queens man sent cash, $10, with specific instructions.

He wanted half to go to a small shopkeeper whose store was looted and half to a social program that would teach unskilled, unemployed young people trades and then help them find decent jobs.

The owner of a two-story building on Utica Avenue in Crown Heights said it didn't matter what the mayor called it. He would be able to collect for the fire damage to one of his tenants, the Thom McAn store. But he still wasn't sure what he would do.

"You see something like this and you wonder how far you can go and for how long before something truly catastrophic happens.

"At first I wanted to walk despite the insurance."

Then he decided he didn't want to be pushed away.

He was encouraged when McAn executives told him that if he rebuilt, they would reopen. Many retail chains had already closed stores in looted neighborhoods.

He was going to try.

The street had been strong; it would be strong again.

The dentist who rented on the second floor felt the same way. "I'm coming back. This is my life. I don't think I should let these two-bit thugs chase me."

There was money around: small grants, large loans, and (for some) insurance. But many merchants didn't have the slightest idea how to get it.

So the head of the American Jewish Committee, who had worked with merchants in Los Angeles after the Watts riot, organized a dozen Business Assistance Teams—BATs—teams of lawyers, bankers, accountants, and teachers who volunteered to staff offices in heavily looted neighborhoods.

They helped merchants reconstruct business records, fill out claim forms and loan applications, and negotiate with underwriters and bankers. In every instance, they encouraged people to hang in. When merchants didn't come in for help, BAT volunteers went out, store to store.

With advice, as with financial aid, a little went a long way.

The owner of Winnie's Designs sold brand-name jeans as well as clothes she made herself. Looters "took it all," she said: "clothes, fabric, money, alterations I was doing for people. Everybody's on my back."

She had just taken out a loan to pay for the jeans.

She needed cash, and though she had insurance, the insurance people were giving her a fit.

"They want me to list every garment," she told a BAT accountant, every pair of jeans and piece of fabric, what was sold, what was looted. She didn't know where to begin.

"You can give them an estimate," the accountant said. "A list of what you had. What was lost. Use receipts and canceled checks. Show them how much you borrowed—$400—to buy the dungarees that were stolen."

"Oh," she said. "Is that how you do it?"

The owner of Capri Furniture didn't have insurance, but he was certain that if the mayor would allow the police to search the neighborhood, door-to-door, he could recover most of his losses without it.

"I know my merchandise is in living rooms within blocks from here," he said. "The police should be given authorization to go and get it out."

41

"History teaches us to make intelligent distinctions," a historian of education wrote in response to the labor historian's essay about the kosher meat rioters.

Or it ought to.

"Notwithstanding conventional wisdom since the 1960s," she wrote, not every riot is an "inarticulate cry for social justice. . . . History offers numerous examples of mass lawlessness"—election-day riots, anti-abolitionist riots, even opera-house riots—"prompted by bigotry, ignorance, greed, and the passions unleashed by mob psychology."

Then there were the riots of July 1863, set in motion by the Civil War draft, particularly the provision that allowed men with $300 to spare to buy themselves out of military service. For four days, rioters—who had numbered in the thousands and were moved by their hatred of Lincoln, their prejudice against blacks, their opposition to the "abolitionist's war," their fear of competition from black laborers, and their hostility toward New York's political and economic elite—burned, looted, and lynched. They even stormed an African-American orphanage. By the time federal troops restored order, rioters had killed at least a dozen black people and left behind a charred, bloody mess.

Most of the rioters were Irishmen who lived in abject poverty. There was no welfare, no public housing, no "public effort" whatsoever to ease their suffering. Still, their suffering was no justification for "barbaric murder." We can understand their "mood without condoning their actions."

There is "a vast moral distinction between purposeful civil disobedience" and the looting of local businesses for resale. To confuse them "demeans those who have struggled for justice." It "ennobles those who steal with no greater end than easy gain." And it slanders "the great majority of poor people, whatever their race or ethnicity, who work hard, respect the rights of their neighbors and know full well the difference between a hoodlum and a dissident."

Readers preferred the historian of education's "moral distinction" to the labor historian's analogy.

The editors of the *Times* preferred the analogy, and though they feared that anything they added might further inflame the passions of their readers, they tried, once more, to bring them around.

So the looters were "animals" and "psychotics" and "welfare cheats," wholly deserving of hatred, denunciation, and jail. Questions remained.

Why were there no looters on Staten Island or Central Park South or in Riverdale? Why only the poorest New Yorkers in the poorest sections of the city? "Why, bluntly, were there no white looters in white neighborhoods?"

Reeling off the elements of their own explanation—poverty, unemployment, discrimination, and deprivation—the editors acknowledged that no single explanation would do.

The historian of education had called for civility as well as for jobs, and the editors agreed that civility was important.

But they refused to believe that race and ethnic origin defined or explained civic virtue.

"Not all, not even many, in the slums became looters. But the looters appeared in slums." Could it be that the civility we prized was related unavoidably to prosperity?

Absolutely not, wrote one reader.

"New York has many poor people, white and non-white—

Chinese, Hasidic Jews and all kinds of European immigrants—none of them looted.

"It appears that civility may be related to something besides prosperity.

"Morality, maybe?"

42

Even the mayor's opponents had to admit that the blackout had energized an anemic reelection campaign. He'd been in the spotlight when everyone else was in the dark, and he had remained in the spotlight with his criticism of Con Edison, lambasting of the looters, and appeals to Washington for aid. Following his lead, people were finally talking about something other than the fiscal crisis and the financial practices that contributed to it (delicate subjects for the mayor, who had formerly been the city comptroller).

Unfortunately, one of the other things people were talking about was the looting, and wherever he went, he was dogged by the charge that he should have asked the governor to send the National Guard.

At the end of July, anticipating an easy day, the mayor drove up to Leibowitz's Pine View, a hotel in the Catskills.

He donned a yarmulke.

Accordionists played "Sidewalks of New York."

Guests fawned.

But not every guest, and at a place where his support should have been as solid as support for the president at a Baptist church in Plains, Georgia, it took only the slightest bit of static to ruin the reception.

One couple expressed great admiration for Abe Beame, the man. But during the blackout, Beame the mayor had disappointed them, and they simply could not vote for him again.

"The police were petrified," one man yelled out, "and the Guard should have been called."

All six of the Democrats challenging the mayor for their party's nomination lambasted the looters. Speaking from the pulpit of the Abyssinian Baptist Church, Manhattan borough president Percy Sutton had called them "marauders and criminals" who didn't care if they dragged "an entire people backward and downward into the primeval ooze and slime of riot and disorder."

And all six criticized the mayor for his handling of that riot and disorder.

But perhaps because he was a long shot with little to lose, Edward Koch hit the mayor first, the most often, and with the most flourish.

"First he lost control of the municipal unions," the congressman charged, "now he has lost control of the streets. . . . He should have had a plan, a plan that included the National Guard."

"Guardsmen are not trained to handle urban riots," the mayor said.

"Guardsmen could have policed the quiet neighborhoods, freeing police up," the congressman said. "Only if the police couldn't handle it themselves would the Guard have gone into looted neighborhoods."

"By the time the Guard arrived, it would have been too late," the mayor said.

"Then the Guard should be abolished."

"It would have been a bloodbath," the mayor said. "By relying on the police . . . we prevented many injuries and probably many deaths."

"Reverse racism," the congressman said. "Everybody . . . knows that if it had been Tiffany's or *The New York Times* that was going to be overrun with two thousand looters . . . and the cops were not able to handle it, you would have wanted the National Guardsmen to protect your property." The congressman said he had spoken with dozens of black and Hispanic businessmen. "Why," they all asked, "did the government fail to do for us what they would have done for every affluent area in this town?"

In retrospect, it is not at all surprising that the congressman's outrage about the looting—outrage that corresponded nicely with his call for the reinstatement of capital punishment in New York—endeared him to an outraged electorate.

But in the weeks after the blackout, as in the weeks before, the pundits, to a man, wrote him off.

"He is still perceived in the boroughs as a crazy liberal from Manhattan," one wrote. "Though Koch tries to change his spots every four years, he is not the image New Yorkers would turn to now."

43

On a television talk show toward the end of July, Con Edison's chairman was asked about the looting.

"We feel badly about it," he said. But not responsible.

Police officials had told him that the "the looting was there, ready to happen, that blackouts don't cause looting." If it hadn't been the blackout, it would have been something else. The chairman added that the city was investigating Con Edison. But who, he wondered, was investigating the city?

Are you saying that the police and fire departments should have been prepared and weren't? a reporter asked afterward. Were they responsible?

"Not at all," the chairman said. "I simply find it interesting and discouraging that public officials who are so anxious to investigate the blackout, which is certainly proper, are not investigating why the rioting occurred."

Public officials continued to investigate.

On the morning of August 4, the chairman of the Federal Power Commission released highlights of the eighty-page report prepared for President Carter. Investigators had concluded that Con Edison's ties to neighboring utilities should have been stronger; protective devices should have been able to withstand lightning; operators should have been better trained to respond to an emergency; and once the system failed, backup generators should have been able to maintain oil pressure in underground cables, thereby speeding restoration. In short, the chairman said, the FPC found "obvious flaws" in the design, planning, and operation of the entire system, flaws that undermined "the ability of the company to provide continuous service without prolonged interruptions."

Two hours later, Con Edison's president responded.

The utility, he said, had already taken many of the steps the FPC had recommended, including the staffing of local generators and substations around the clock. In some instances, it had gone beyond the commission's recommendations. For example, it had initiated a review of the breaker settings at substations throughout Westchester.

But Con Ed's president rejected the commission's characterization of the utility's planning and operation, and he insisted that an extensive, time-consuming, and expensive redesign of the system was absolutely unnecessary.

"Never before in the history of our system," he said, "have we lost even one double-circuit 345-kilovolt line to a single stroke of lightning."

On July 13, "we lost two."

"We would all perhaps like to think that we could point to one thing or person to explain the blackout and a restoration of service that took up to twenty-five hours to complete," said the FPC chairman.

But we can't point to one thing or one person.

It was "a series of incidents, a number of mechanical inadequacies, insufficient inter-ties and start-up capacity on those inter-ties, inadequate operating procedures at various stages, too much reliance on manual switches during the restoration, and a need for auxiliary power to maintain pressure in underground cable."

44

"Soon the rats and the roaches are going to own this place," said a young Bushwick man. His mother had just returned from a walk to the pharmacy, only to find that it was still closed.

"This is going to be a ghost town. The blackout has paved the way."

The president of the Urban League urged the president to come to New York.

As a candidate, the president had spoken with feeling about the problems of the urban poor and promised that a Democratic administration would help. But as president, he spoke mostly about the need for balanced budgets and austerity; about government waste, unnecessary regulation, and red tape.

African-Americans, who voted for him in overwhelming numbers in a close election, felt betrayed.

"We have no full-employment policy," the president of the Urban League said. "We have no welfare reform policy. We have no national health policy. We have no aggressive affirmative-action policy. We have no national solutions to the grinding problems of poverty and discrimination.

"It will take many millions of dollars to repair the damage, but the same resources placed into employment and housing improvement programs may well have prevented it."

The streets of Bushwick were littered with the burned-black remains of buildings, piles of garbage, and glass.

On two blocks of Broadway, not a single store had reopened. On a third, there was a lone ice-cream shop.

"Who is going to be first?" asked the owner of that shop, who said the retail merchants were all peering out their windows, waiting to see who else would open. "No one wants to be the first."

The SBA was waiting, too, said the owner of Al-Bert's. It was extremely reluctant to make loans to merchants in a neighborhood that had sunk so low.

Before the blackout, many New Yorkers had not even heard of Bushwick. Now they knew it, as they knew the South Bronx, as a synonym for urban blight.

Residents were afraid to go out at night. They were also afraid to sleep. Some families slept in shifts. Others put ladders by their windows before they went to bed.

The head of the Municipal Assistance Corporation, the state agency established in 1975 to oversee the city's finances, invited the president to New York.

Founded by Peter Stuyvesant in the middle of the seventeenth century, Bushwick had been a Dutch farming community until the middle of the nineteenth century, when thousands of Germans arrived and began to build three-story houses and big breweries. In no time, Bushwick's 1,146 acres were the center of the metropolitan area's booming beer industry. Russians, English, Irish, and Poles added to the mix in the late nineteenth century, and then Italians in huge numbers in the 1930s and 1940s. But Prohibition and the Depression had resulted in the ruin of half the breweries, and labor troubles and high costs in the postwar years had encouraged the relocation of several others to the South and West. The Brooklyn Navy Yard, which had employed thousands, closed in 1966.

There goes the neighborhood, some said in the 1950s, when

African-Americans started to arrive from the rural South and from overcrowded tenements in Harlem. But anyone who had been paying attention knew that the neighborhood was already well on its way to gone.

The editors of *The New York Times* invited the president to New York.

They had already taken him to task for his initial response to the blackout, the technocratic talk of energy policy and power grids: "A President does not worry about generator nuts and bolts when the social fabric of the nation's largest city is exposed as inflammable." A president cannot confine himself to relieving tension in Korea or negotiating peace in the Middle East "when life's losers are rampaging in the streets of America, spreading blight and the disease of racism."

The president's subsequent comments about unemployment were encouraging, but there was more he could do.

He could come to New York.

See the devastation.

Talk to the looters and the looted.

Use the occasion to encourage the nation to assume some of the responsibilities it had dumped upon its oldest cities, especially the cost of welfare. Or launch a national youth corps to train thousands of idle young people and put them to work rebuilding their neighborhoods and their lives.

What happened next was ugly but not unique to Bushwick.

Real estate brokers began to scare people out of the neighborhood with (self-fulfilling) prophecies of decline, of encroaching poverty and crime. Some of those prophecies came in phone calls in the middle of the night.

Banks stopped granting mortgages.

Speculators bought houses cheap and sold them dear to people who couldn't afford to own them but whose home loans, conveniently arranged by the sellers, were backed by the federal government. When buyers defaulted, speculators collected the inflated value, and the government boarded up the houses (thereby encouraging additional flight from the neighborhood). Or it allowed speculators to sell the foreclosed houses again, a process that might have gone on indefinitely, except that buyers who couldn't afford their mortgage payments couldn't afford to maintain their homes. Before long, whole blocks of Bushwick's houses were boarded up, beyond resale or repair.

Meanwhile, owners of apartment buildings, taking advantage of another well-intentioned government program, rented to welfare recipients for rents that were well above market rates. Owners regularly subdivided their property, but rarely maintained it. The only work landlords did on their property was subdivision, and when apartments became uninhabitable, tenants moved (sometimes to another of their landlord's buildings) and landlords abandoned buildings or paid people to burn them to the ground.

In 1960, Bushwick was 70 percent white. In 1977 it was more than 70 percent black and Puerto Rican.

And it was on fire.

New York's junior senator invited the president to New York. "I wish he'd come with me to see the South Bronx," he said. There he could see "something that has never happened before in the history of urban settlements—the disappearance of a once great neighborhood. . . . If you ever see what's happening there, it knocks simple ideas out of your head once and for all."

Bushwick seemed to have hit bottom, but even in the aftermath of the blackout, it was a more complicated place than the people who used the name to say "inner city," "ghetto," "drugs," "crime," "black," and "poor" could understand.

Although many Italian-Americans had left for Queens and

Long Island, those who remained sustained a vibrant community in northeast Bushwick.

African-Americans and Latinos with decent jobs lived in decent yellow brick apartment buildings and, despite rising prices and stagnant wages, struggled to climb into the middle class. Those who had already made it lived on tree-lined streets, a few of those streets gaslit. Some of them lived in brownstones right in the center of Bushwick, a stone's throw from blocks of apartments that landlords had abandoned to drug dealers and blocks of Broadway, once bustling, where now there was not a single open store. There was only one way to "size it up," said a physical therapist who lived in one of the brownstones on Linden Avenue: "It's like having a cutthroat class in school side by side with a class that is willing to learn."

The *Daily News*'s Washington columnist—noting that the president had plans to travel to Mississippi—invited him to New York.

The president had scheduled a town meeting at the home of a fertilizer manufacturer in Yazoo City. He wanted to keep in touch with ordinary Americans.

A "laudable goal," the columnist thought, to get out of Washington, to "hear firsthand" people's complaints, to learn firsthand their hopes, fears, and dreams. But he should come to New York instead.

The message he would get "from small-town America, north or south," was likely to be "more reassuring" and "less relevant" than the message awaiting him in the South Bronx, Harlem, or Bedford-Stuyvesant.

Bushwick was a story. Savvy reporters went out to get it.

They saw some streets that looked like Brooklyn Heights, and others that looked like Dresden in 1945.

They listened as some residents attributed the looting to

morals, and others—including (much to their surprise) some merchants—attributed it to unemployment.

But when they asked people what the neighborhood needed to survive, they all agreed: a massive cleanup, including the razing of every abandoned building (empty lots would be better); around-the-clock police protection; a crackdown on drug dealers; and jobs.

When reporters asked merchants if they were going to stick it out, many took offense.

"I like it here."

"These are my people."

"I have earned my bread here."

"After a while you get a special feeling about a place. Besides, why should we give our homes up to the bad elements?"

The president, said the president's press secretary, had no plans to visit New York anytime soon.

45

"The morals of piranha are especially unpleasant when adopted by people," wrote a widely syndicated columnist, who thought the idea that hunger had caused the looting (in the city with the nation's most generous welfare payments) was nonsense.

But, he argued, such nonsense was not new.

The "attempt to legitimize" looting began in the 1960s, when progressives, including those appointed to several presidential commissions, concluded that riots in Watts, Newark, and Detroit were best understood as "spontaneous" protests "against injustice."

Scholars who studied those riots found otherwise. One study characterized the Detroit riot as "a collective celebration," a "carnival, during which about forty liquor stores were broken into and much liquor consumed." Two-thirds of the looters had already been convicted of crimes. One-third had been convicted of major crimes. They had paid no attention whatsover to who owned the stores.

The columnist recognized that occasionally rioters had rioted to express indignation or to advance a principle. But, citing the research of a Harvard sociologist, he concluded that much more often they had rioted for "fun and profit." When the ambassador to the United Nations said that hunger had caused the looting, he was simply justifying it.

When he said that it would have happened anywhere, including Switzerland, he was saying that it was natural.

But it wasn't natural, and it wouldn't have happened in Switzerland, because the United States had something in its cities that Switzerland did not. It had "many people who lack the economic abilities and character traits necessary for life in a free and lawful society."

Animals, rabble, parasites, and piranha.

A *New York Times* columnist didn't think there was any mystery about those words.

"Everyone knew they were about race."

A prominent social critic, writing in *Commentary*, thought the metaphor needed to be refined. To "anyone watching" the looters "at work, surging out of the shadows in a horde and scurrying back into the cover of darkness as the police cars came by, the imagery suggested is one taken from insect life—from urban insect life—rather than the jungle or forest."

Animals trample, but New Yorkers did not feel trampled.

They felt as if they had been "given a sudden glimpse into the foundation" of their house and had "seen, with horror, that it was utterly infested and rotting away."

Whatever the epithet, wrote the *Times* columnist, its meaning was clear.

"Blacks as a group are not like us."

They are "inferior."

They are certainly not like "our grandparents," who had nothing but got ahead by working hard.

But when "our grandparents" had nothing, they had jobs.

"They didn't know 40 to 60 percent unemployment, let alone 86 percent for teenagers. Those who call the looters animals should try to imagine what it is like to live in poverty in a society that, perhaps more than any other in history, exalts material wealth and consumption."

The social critic thought the problem of unemployment was too knotty for the liberal mind to grasp.

No doubt that "hordes" of teenagers and young men passed their days "on street corners," engaged in "a form of play" that consisted "largely of offering menace to one another and to passers-by."

No doubt they were "idle" and "headed for trouble."

But it was not at all clear that they minded being idle, or that they were poor.

And "the idea" that they were "unemployed—in the sense of having sought and failed to find a job"—seemed "in many cases simply a laughable proposition."

For many, it did not "pay to take a job." Welfare kept them housed and fed. Or women. What's more, beyond the most menial labor, there wasn't much they were qualified to do. Why should they settle for the minimum wage when they could make real money running numbers or selling drugs, when they could steal, pimp, or mug?

The liberals wanted the president to give them jobs. Real jobs. Some of them demanded jobs themselves.

But, the social critic wrote, "one pays those young men less than proper respect to imagine that President Carter can so easily afford the means to buy them away from their present life."

"Moralistic bilge," wrote the editor of *Dissent*.

Since the blackout, there had been a "tide" of it, popular and intellectual: policemen and taxi drivers calling the looters animals; "former liberals decrying the breakdown of morality and responsibility and social order." Despite the fall of Richard Nixon, it was clear that the temper of his times—meanness (masquerading as morality); middle-class selfishness; sly, implicit, nastiness—still reigned.

Life is unfair, the president said.

And government could not do anything about it.

Poverty and unemployment don't excuse antisocial behavior, they all said.

Well of course they don't excuse it. The question is whether they help us understand it.

The editor reminded readers that unemployment among black youths was at least 50 percent. Housing was "wretched." Poverty persisted. Neglect and callousness had produced "social demoralization strongly alloyed with pathology." Black leaders were at a loss.

Jobs alone, he admitted, would not bring health to the city's streets. The malaise and despair were too great. But the blackout had cost the city hundreds of millions of dollars. What if that money (or even a fraction of the money spent on defense) went to jobs instead?

The alternatives? Send neocons to 125th Street to preach fiscal responsibility? Hand out tougher sentences? Build thicker walls around the ghettoes, and more jails?

The editors of the *Amsterdam News* had heard many people say, "While we don't condone the violence, the real problem is jobs."

Too many. They believed it was not enough not to condone the violence. "We must forthrightly and adamantly condemn it," they wrote in a page-one editorial that all of New York's other papers either reprinted or reported as news.

Observing that no urban crime was as common as the crime black people committed against other black people, the editors argued that even the slightest implication that the black community accepted "joblessness" as a justification for looting—particularly the looting of black-owned stores—was evidence of a "self-destructive," "suicidal" tolerance of "lawlessness, abuse, and violence."

The editors conceded that "white-dominated city, state, and

federal governments had failed totally and completely to comprehend the depth of despair" among young black people; that black leaders had lost touch with ordinary black people, especially black youth; and that jobs would help enormously.

"But," the editors concluded, "our kids need inspiration and motivation and direction as badly as they need jobs." And no government failure, no failure of black leadership, no disappointment, betrayal, or neglect justified the looting.

It was "criminal, outrageous and damnable. It's taken us too long to get where we are to accept such destructive behavior now."

To understand the looting was not to excuse it, the *Times* columnist insisted.

Nor was it to underestimate the "fear and outrage" generated by "lawlessness."

It was simply, and honestly, to recognize that "blacks in our major cities have special disabilities, the expectable result of a history of slavery and segregation and dislocation."

Neither hatred nor bigotry was "likely to advance the cause of law or the safety of the middle-class majority. We can build walls and arm ourselves with guns and shoot suspected lawbreakers on sight, but we shall not find social peace."

It was cant to talk about unemployment, the social critic wrote.

And cant to talk about poverty, desperation, invisibility, racial oppression, and (hundreds of social programs and billions of dollars later) indifference, apathy, and neglect.

It was cant—and it was ludicrous—to say, as a *New Yorker* writer had said, that the attitude toward the riots had caused the riots.

And "above all," it was cant to say, as one historian had said, that the looters were sending us a "pained message." Anyone who had seen them knew that "they were having the time of their lives."

So why did they loot?

They sensed an unusual opportunity.

They found strength in numbers.

And they believed that they had permission.

In that belief, they were correct. Liberals—in the media, in the government, in the arts—gave them permission. All the people who had made "race and poverty" legitimate "excuses for lawlessness."

Pained messages? They came from liberal attitudes and progressive social policy, and they came "more subtly but just as surely as from any old-time Southern sheriff."

You are inferior.

You can't be held to traditional standards for the grades you get in school or the work you do on the job.

You can't be expected to be husbands to your wives and fathers to your children.

You are not responsible for your crimes.

You are children or, "ironically," animals: "not fully enough human to be held morally responsible for your own behavior."

The social critic concluded that the looters were "neither innocents nor savages" but "people in the grip of a pathology that arises from moral chaos. They were doing something they knew to be wrong but had been given a license for, and had not been able to find the inner resources to overcome their temptation."

"Why no white looters in white neighborhoods?" the editors of *The New York Times* had asked.

The social critic thought she knew.

"The real answer," she wrote, was not to be found in the economy or even the heat but rather "in a decade's worth of the spread of this very liberal and very racist idea: that being black is a condition for special moral allowance."

46

On Sunday, August 7, the mayor's press office issued a press release. Applications for two thousand federally funded blackout cleanup jobs would be distributed at regional Manpower centers the following day. To be eligible, you had to be eighteen, out of work, or in a family with a low income, and live in an area hit by looting or arson.

The jobs would pay $30 a day for thirty-three days.

No one arrested during the blackout would be hired.

The press release was accurate in every detail but one: It instructed hopefuls to report to one of seven regional Manpower offices, when it should have instructed them to report to the nearest neighborhood employment office, of which there were twice as many.

People began gathering at the Brooklyn Manpower office late Sunday, and all through the night, the crowd grew. Those who left for the office at daybreak, expecting to be among the first to arrive, were frustrated to find a long line.

When the director arrived shortly before eight, there were thousands of people in the street. He called the police.

The crowd continued to grow, with pushing and a few scuffles. Several people tried to climb up into the building. Others tore down a gate.

"This is what we go through," said an unemployed handyman, who had been in line since three a.m. "You people in white collars messed it up for us. We want a job."

The deputy mayor for employment, who happened to be in the Brooklyn Manpower office that Monday morning, wanted to go into the crowd to apologize for the mistake.

Her colleagues talked her out of it. Instead, she grabbed a bullhorn and pleaded for patience from a second-story window.

A few people hurled rocks her way; the rest were patient.

A few minutes later, police began to distribute applications.

"My heart bleeds for these people," the deputy mayor said. "Here they are fighting over crumbs. We have over 300,000 unemployed in the city, not counting youngsters, and we don't have enough jobs."

By afternoon, photocopies of applications were selling on the street for $2 apiece.

The small staff at the Manpower office on East 149th Street in the Bronx didn't even have applications. When the director asked people to report to the employment office nearest their homes, one group of youths tore down the gates outside the office. By the time police restored order, a staff member had lost her purse, a police inspector had lost his watch and part of his shirt, and three people had been hurt.

The crowds in Queens and Staten Island were slightly smaller, the frustrations much the same. One woman had traveled eight miles to get to the Jamaica Manpower office, her twin five-year-old boys in tow.

She arrived at five a.m. After three hours, she learned she was in front of the wrong office. She and the boys walked two miles to the right one.

"I am dying to get a job," she said, "and I had no one to leave my youngsters with. Believe me, welfare is no fun."

A twenty-eight-year-old who had worked as a shipping clerk until he was laid off in January said he wanted a job so he wouldn't have to steal. Until he found one, he was living with a friend. "Puerto Ricans and blacks do care about working," he said. "I would like to have a decent job so I could think about getting married and raising a family."

Two thousand people showed up in East Harlem.

Officials anxiously announced the bad news.

The crowd dispersed, though not before one group of youths broke a few windows and tore down the front door.

By Thursday morning, most of the neighborhood employment offices had been accepting applications for two and a half days.

The lines were as long as they had been on Monday.

"I've been doing illegal things all my life," said a twenty-year-old waiting in Harlem. "I've supported myself by picking up numbers and selling reefers. I would do a lot of favors for people. If your car got stolen, I would steal you another one. I want to do something legitimate."

In Brooklyn, fifteen hundred people—some of whom had spent the night—waited in line outside the Bedford armory. Across the street, hundreds more (standing on sidewalks, sitting in cars, on cars, and on curbs) waited to get in that line, even though it did not appear to be moving.

"They throw us crumbs and let us fight over them like birds," complained a twenty-four-year-old who had been in line for three days and out of work for two years. "We're fighting over jobs that only last thirty-three days."

Inside the armory, the regional director of the Department of Employment was at his wit's end. But he was completely sympathetic. "It's like giving an aspirin to a cancer patient," he said. "At least it shows you these people really want to work."

47

At the end of August, Con Edison completed the second phase of its investigation, and the company president met with reporters to discuss the findings.

There was lightning on the evening of July 13, he said. But investigators had concluded that the system should have been able to withstand it. Mechanical failure and human error were ultimately to blame for the blackout.

The president identified several examples of mechanical failure, including circuit breakers that did not close and backup generators that broke down. But he placed special emphasis on the actions of the system operator.

Early in the sequence, thinking he had other options, he did not take aggressive action to reclose feeders and increase local generation. Had he increased in-city generation more rapidly, he would have reduced the load on the remaining ties and might well have prevented the tripping of the last two 345-kilovolt feeders. Later on, unaware of the exact condition of the system, he did not act to reduce voltage or shed load soon enough to prevent the overloading of the ties to New Jersey and Long Island.

The president said that the system operator had been moved to a staff job. But when a reporter asked if there were likely to be other personnel changes, he responded angrily.

"You're talking about blame here. We're not looking for blame. We're not out to blame a relay, or a circuit breaker, or an operator, or a designer, or an official, or even the outside agencies that have prevented us from building the facilities we want. What we're trying to do now is to put together the things that we know will work, and make the system better."

48

The Brooklyn district attorney summoned reporters.

His office had statistics that shed light on the backgrounds of the first 176 looters indicted on felony charges.

Reporters rushed back to their offices with the news.

"Nearly half of Brooklyn's looters had full-time jobs," reported the *New York Post* in its afternoon edition. The following morning, both the *Daily News* and *The New York Times* rounded the number up to half. All three papers reported that few looters—8.5 percent—were on welfare.

The Brooklyn DA said that his "hard facts" appeared to belie much speculation about the looting and looters, including "statements made earlier by President Carter and others that the looting had been committed by hungry people."

All the reporters agreed. "The numbers," wrote a reporter for the *Daily News*, "appeared to refute earlier reports that the majority of the looters were jobless and needed food for their families."

In the rush from press conference to print, reporters didn't have time to check the DA's facts, let alone analyze them.

They didn't notice that the DA had bungled the numbers. Then they themselves, or their editors, made bad math worse, exaggerating the average income and the number of people for whom there was income information. It wasn't half but just over a quarter of the indicted looters who had told the court they were fully employed.

Furthermore, in their headlines and in their articles, editors and reporters noted the number of looters on welfare as if it were remarkable. But most of the looters were single young men, and few single young men were on welfare.

Finally, they failed to note—if in fact they grasped—the actual size of the sample: not the first 176 indicted looters, as reported, but the 46 indicted looters for whom the Brooklyn DA's office had income data. Those 46 were 4 percent of the looters arrested in Brooklyn, and 1 percent of the looters overall.

The deputy mayor for criminal justice had also been crunching numbers. But when he released his survey of arrested looters, citywide, he cautioned reporters not to draw sweeping conclusions.

His survey, he said, was of those arrested, not convicted.

His data did not allow for an analysis of employment by type.

And his comparisons were of looters to everyone arrested for any crime in previous months, not to people arrested for similar crimes.

"The first comprehensive survey of suspects seized citywide in the looting," wrote a *New York Times* reporter, "shows that 45 percent of the adults arrested had jobs—an employment rate half again as high as the rate among those normally arrested for crimes in New York City." The survey also showed that "only 10 percent were on welfare." Like the Brooklyn DA's survey, the statistics "seemed to contradict statements made by President Carter and others that the looters were largely people who were jobless and hungry."

The deputy mayor had cautioned against sweeping conclusions, but he didn't mention the biggest problem with his numbers: Like the DA's, they were based on interviews conducted between arrest and arraignment by the Pretrial Services Agency. Agency staff used those interviews to make recommendations for bail.

Whether or not arrestees had jobs, most understood they would have a much better chance of getting released on bail, or even on their own recognizance, if they said they did.

The agency ordinarily tried to verify the information arrestees provided. But with thousands of people arrested, and mayhem in the courthouses, staffers were able to verify the employment status of only 3 percent of the people they interviewed.

49

City, state, and federal investigators were as skeptical of Con Edison's talk of "human and mechanical error" as they had been of its talk of lightning.

They jumped all over the utility's second report.

They insisted that the utility should not and could not blame the blackout on one individual (or even several) and a few faulty pieces of equipment. The utility had hired those individuals and trained them; it had designed the network and the control room; it had purchased the generators, transformers, and protective devices and was supposed to have maintained them; it had devised emergency procedures and restoration plans.

Con Edison executives bore first and last responsibility for Con Edison's performance. If the network did not function as it was designed to function, or if (as the Federal Power Commission suggested in its preliminary report) the network was not designed well to begin with, executives had no one to blame but themselves.

50

As the city prepared to give away the last of its emergency grants, officials estimated that three-quarters of the looted stores had reopened.

One of them was the Radio Clinic.

Six weeks after the owner watched looters empty his store, he watched workmen install a new storefront.

He'd received a grant from the emergency aid fund while waiting to collect insurance and close on an SBA loan.

It wasn't much, but he was grateful.

"I think the city did a fantastic job with what was available," he said.

Three-quarters citywide did not mean three-quarters of the stores in every neighborhood. The fraction was much smaller in East Harlem, and those store owners who did reopen were preyed upon by arsonists and thieves.

Still, the owner of Morris Toyland refused to give up. He would have had a good excuse: After thirty years in the neighborhood, he had been planning to retire.

Not now.

"I will not retire owing people," he said.

He and a few of his neighbors chipped in to pay for an armed guard, who patrolled after hours.

And he borrowed nearly $200,000 from the SBA. "People in the neighborhood keep thinking the merchants make money on the looting. I tell them no. No one is giving us money. I have to borrow over more years than are left in my life."

He did not want to let down his employees, or all the other good people, the vast majority of people, in the neighborhood.

They have been good to me, he said.

"Now it's a matter of having to stay in so I can get out the right way."

Under pressure from city officials and industry regulators, insurance underwriters stopped quibbling over the difference between a burglary and a riot. Store owners who had fire insurance with a riot rider collected, including the owner of Merchants. An adjuster came by; the company paid full value.

He also collected $6,000 or $7,000 on his government policy: $1,000 for the blackout and $1,000 for each of the break-ins in late July and August.

"They kept coming in," the owner said. "You couldn't keep them out. I put in guard dogs. They terrorized them, sprayed them with aerosol cans, kidnapped one and ransomed him back to the security company. The dogs were worthless."

He went back to the neighborhood a few times, but after thirty years, "it wasn't easy. I found it hard to look at the place, next to impossible to go in."

The break-ins after the blackout removed his remaining doubts. He bought a new store in Jackson Heights, Queens. It was "smaller, but large enough to make a living."

Standing in the shell of his store the day of the blackout, the owner of Superior Furniture had sworn that after twenty-seven years, he would not be back.

By September he was back, with $80,000 worth of new merchandise.

"My greed got the best of me."

He wasn't doing the business he once had.

Who was? The South Bronx had lost a hundred thousand people since 1970.

"There is no more frosting on the cake," he said. "But we are still making a profit."

51

"Why did you do it?" asked the wife of the Bushwick man arrested outside the Flatbush Avenue clothing store.

"Because everybody was doing it," said the seventeen-year-old from Harlem.

Everybody was getting it: "ladies," "grown ladies," old men, little kids.

It was right next door.

Nobody was getting caught.

"I was out there 'cause I'm a poor person," said the looter from Brownsville.

Not "poverty-stricken" but "poor."

"I can't afford the things I want."

She said she wouldn't loot jewelry or furniture. "I don't do that kind of stealing."

But her family was on welfare, and welfare gave them only enough to get by, to survive, nothing more.

She was happy to get food for her mother and diapers for her son. Her mother was happy, too.

"I mean, I wouldn't just go out and just start ripping people off like that," he said.

He had thought about a life of crime, but it wasn't for him. It was "too dangerous," and he didn't like "the retirement plan:

The only thing you're guaranteed with a life of crime is your death.

"But it was an opportunity, you know, it was like a gift. It was like the man upstairs said, 'I'm gonna put out the lights for twenty-four hours and you all go off . . . and get everything you can. Those who get caught, get caught. Those who don't, well, more power to you.' "

"Why?" the wife of the Bushwick man asked him.

He had spent eight days in jail, and the worst part was not the heat, the food, or the company (which was on the wild side) but the fear: fear that he was going to lose his job.

"For what?" she asked. Women's pants and blouses.

He told the judge he had no money, which got him a free lawyer; he told his boss that it was all a big mistake.

She kept asking.

"I feel it was wrong," the seventeen-year-old said. "I know it was wrong, but I don't feel too bad about it, because that's the way it is sometimes."

Under normal circumstances, said the looter from Brownsville, "I wouldn't loot. I'm not that type of person. I was raised—I was taught better than that because I know stealing is wrong, looting is wrong, but when the blackout came, there was a lot of things I needed, a lot of things . . . my family lacks."

She hadn't given any thought to the race of the store owners. She didn't care now.

"That have nothing to do about it," she said.

"I'm not prejudiced."

He didn't think about it that night. Reading and thinking about it afterward, he figured that even though some stores might have had "black managers," most were owned by whites.

"As long as we didn't burn up the stores," they were going to "get it all back, claiming it on their insurance and claiming it on their taxes."

They'll "put in new windows.

"Put the stuff right back into the stores.

"Be right back in business the next day."

The Bushwick man regretted the night, but mostly because he got caught.

He was a cyclist, and he had always wanted a nice bike. He made a decent living selling clothes, but besides Catholic school for his son and a Buick, there was no money to spare. That's why he had ridden to Flatbush Avenue.

"I saw an opportunity and took advantage of it."

He didn't start the looting.

He didn't organize a group or pry off a gate.

He didn't stick up or mug anyone.

"It was as if there was a wallet on the ground and money sticking out of it and no one around."

The seventeen-year-old felt bad about some store owners but figured they'd collect on insurance. About others, she couldn't have cared less. "The man on the corner, I didn't like him anyway. He was too cheap, he wouldn't give nobody no credit."

"A lot of the looters were people who wouldn't normally do something like that," the Brownsville looter said. Some were welfare recipients living in city housing, not because they wanted to but because they had no choice. They were deprived of things they needed. They saw a way to get those things, and they went out and got them, "not because they're thieves, not because they mind working," but because "self-preservation is the law of nature. Opportunity arrived."

If she had thought the nice store owners would not get back their money, she would have felt bad. And she did feel bad about losing the good stores: "After the blackout, we had to go pretty far to go to the store."

"Some of the looters had jobs," he said, but "they're not making enough money to support their family the way they feel their family should be living." They needed to have "two or three things going at one time." That was how people looked at the blackout. It was another "way of getting over." They saw "the chance to get things that . . . it would take them years and years to get."

And that's how it was with him. If a guy came up and asked him to break into a store, he would ask the guy if he was crazy. But with the lights out, there was little risk.

"I mean, if a guy came around here with a truck full of food and he was dumb enough to get out of his truck and go upstairs in the building and leave his truck open."

The Bushwick looter's wife didn't get it.
She was mad.
She kept asking him why he did it, why.
"It was," he said, "as if I'd stolen something from her."

They didn't loot in 1965 "because the crisis wasn't too bad," said the seventeen-year-old. "People had jobs then and . . . they didn't do too bad; the city wasn't low of money, but now . . . everybody's out of a job almost, and you know everybody's down for stealing."

In 1965 his mother wouldn't let him out of the house.
But "times have changed.

"They are much blacker."

His brothers and sisters, as young now as he was then, went out.

"She was harder on me than she is on all the younger kids now. But, you know, she was younger and the way the . . . world looked on you was different than the way it looks on you now. People raised children differently in '77 than you did in '65. The people, the country, went through a complete change . . . you got more people in power, you know, moral standards that went lower . . . much lower."

"No, I don't think I would" do it again, she said. "I would be scared this time because I know they lost so much money that they would be ready."

"It would depend on the situation," he said, "and what I was doing at the time the blackout came."

The decision wouldn't turn on money so much as his "position in life."

He wanted to go to college and law school. If "I were in law school" or "established in a firm," making "more in a month or just as much in a month . . . or probably more in a couple of months than what I made out there . . . I wouldn't take the risk of getting busted for looting and having to go to jail and blowing my schooling."

The Bushwick man was surprised that his wife was so surprised. He didn't understand it. "I just took a chance. I don't know anyone who's really gotten anywhere and didn't take a chance. Rockefeller and Getty—you know what their fathers were all about. Their fathers were murderers and thieves. They took a chance, they just got over."

———

She was not optimistic. "It's getting worse; I don't think it's getting better." Nothing was going to change, she said, until people had jobs.

Sure enough, he said, the looted businesses were back open. Except those set on fire. That was "really wrong." The stealing was one thing, but "some people was just out there being destructive . . . tearing down beyond repair," "burning down stores," "hurting people purposely."

"People didn't have to bust up or burn or hurt people." When they did, "they started really hurting themselves. We was losing then, because that was taking money out of the neighborhood."

But, he said, "some people just don't give a fuck about other people." They have no "sense" and no "self-control . . . They don't give a damn."

But she was seventeen and not without hope.

The governor had come through with a job last summer. Perhaps the president would come through now.

"I never would say that we was right for what we did," said the Brownsville looter, but "people don't think about right or wrong when they got a chance to get what they need . . . I mean, it's really a heavy thing when you get down to it . . . it's all up to the human mind. Everyone thinks a different way, as you know. It's all up to the individual that's out there doing what he's doing at that time."

52

In the city, people did what city people do.

They worked.

They walked.

They listened. They talked.

They ran numbers.

They swam laps.

They smashed car windows and returned to find their windows smashed.

The lightning had struck a tower standing between substations in Millwood West and Buchanan South. The 345-kilovolt lines on that tower, like all power lines, were equipped with protective devices, which for the sake of simplicity are often referred to by their most familiar component, circuit breakers. Circuit breakers, activated by relays, are designed to isolate parts of the power grid in the event of dramatic power surpluses or deficits. The breakers open the circuit and gauge the surplus, deficit, or damage. If all is well, the breakers reclose. When they are working properly, they open and close so quickly that no one besides substation and Control Center operators monitoring meters, which look like oscilloscopes, know they have opened in the first place. If they don't close in a specified period of time, a backup system kicks in, interrupting the circuits that feed the line in trouble.

People waited in long lines for *Star Wars*, even though it was four months old, and play-off tickets, after the Yankees finished atop the American League East for the second year in a row.

Kids who had looted helped the owner of Sylvester's clean up his store.

Others threatened the owner of a Broadway stereo shop: Next time, they said, we'll "loot you" even more.

Twenty-year-olds, heads full of early Marx, late Marcuse, and all of Hoffman, shoplifted from supermarkets and department stores; they thought private property was theft; they loathed the system.

Police captured Son of Sam, though not until after he had claimed another victim.

When lightning struck that tower, protective relays automatically opened circuit breakers at Millwood West and Buchanan South, interrupting the flow of power from Indian Point. With no source for its power, Indian Point Number 3 shut down.

Under ordinary circumstances, the circuits then would have reclosed. But the manufacturers of turbine generators had recently warned customers about the damage done to generator shafts by rapid openings and closings, stops and starts. In early July engineers had adjusted circuit-breaker controls at Buchanan North and South to reduce the possibility of rapid openings and closings until they could install new breaker control relays.

The lines between Buchanan South and Millwood West did not close.

At the same time, a poorly designed protective circuit at Buchanan South caused a breaker failure timer to open the 345-kilovolt line between Buchanan and Ladentown, one of two major ties across the Hudson River.

That left one tie, two circuits, to the west; two additional lines running on a tower from Buchanan to Sprain Brook; and, most important, the right fork of the city's power grid: the 345-kilovolt lines that ran from Millwood to Pleasant Valley, lines that tied Con Ed to upstate New York and New England power pools.

Street vendors hawked a hot new T-shirt; WHERE WERE YOU? it read.

Grateful WINS executives gave every employee on duty during the blackout a small red Eveready flashlight with the station's logo affixed, backward, to the lens.

"Complete bullshit," one reporter said.

People arranged kickbacks. People rigged bids.

Pickpockets picked pockets, and people had their pockets picked.

At Con Edison's Energy Control Center—the block-long concrete bunker on West End Avenue where a hundred operators, dispatchers, engineers, and technicians worked (in three shifts) around the clock—the system operator sent out an alarm to operators at every plant in the city, requiring them to increase generation. He ordered the Astoria operator to fire up gas turbines that were not on line. By 8:55 he had made up about a third of the power he had lost.

A minute later, a second stroke of lightning struck a second tower and knocked out two more lines, one that ran between Buchanan North and Sprain Brook and one that ran between Millwood West and Sprain Brook.

Breakers opened at Buchanan North, Millwood West, Eastview, and Sprain Brook, clearing the fault. They reclosed at Millwood West and Sprain Brook, and the line between those two stations went right back into service. But breakers did not reclose at Buchanan North, opening the last line to the west; and the loss of the line between Buchanan and Sprain Brook caused a spike on the line between Millwood and Pleasant Valley. A slightly bent metal contact caused a faulty response to that spike, tripping one of two main lines to the north.

In a matter of minutes, the city had lost four of five of its lines to the north and west, half its power.

People tried to pay inspectors—of buildings, of restaurants, of low-income mortgage applications, of nursing homes—to look the other way.

Some looked the other way; some refused.

Estimates of the cost of the blackout ran to $350 million, not counting lost production time, retail sales, and tax revenues.

People planned business trips, and people padded expense reports for trips they had taken in May and June.

The Mets lost ninety-eight games and finished last in the National League East.

Homeless people looked for places to sleep.

The system operator knew he had lost power from the north.

He didn't know how much power he had lost, where he had lost it, or why, and he didn't have a lot of time, let alone peace of mind, for investigation.

He and his team had to make sure the power they did have was evenly distributed.

They had to figure how much power they could pick up locally, and how much New Jersey and Long Island could provide.

And, if all else failed, they had to figure out when to begin shedding load manually, cutting off power to customers, starting in neighborhoods without high-rises—to save the system. But even if they had known exactly how much, where, and why, they would have been reluctant to cut people's power.

In the Control Center of a utility infamous for its blackouts and brownouts, the first commandment was "Thou Shalt Not Shed Load."

The city began to demolish Bushwick's abandoned buildings and fill potholes.

The federal government talked of building a housing project that Nixon had put on hold.

A year after the blackout, nine out of ten looted Broadway businesses remained closed.

Private investors talked of a shopping mall or a center for light industry in the old Rheingold Brewery.

Thousands marched in solidarity with Soviet Jewry.

The Control Center's windowless rooms were equipped with meters, switchboards, CRTs, lights, teletypes, diagrams, phones, maps, buzzers, alarms, and floor-to-ceiling wall displays. Unlike many other control centers, including the New York power pool control center, just outside of Albany, Con Edison's was not equipped with a single dynamic display of the entire system: generation, transmission lines, transformers, relays, and breakers.

Without a dynamic display, the system operator's knowledge was piecemeal. He didn't know the Buchanan North breakers were open, because he didn't see the teletype delivering that news. Therefore, he didn't know the line running from Buchanan North to Ramapo—the second and last line across the Hudson River—was out.

The Control Center's Westchester district operator knew, from a flashing screen and a piercing alarm, about the breakers and the line. But he was in one room, and the system operator and power dispatcher were in another, and for reasons that were never made clear, they were not talking.

People paid people for protection, and people punished people who refused to pay.

The president came to New York and visited rubble-strewn

Charlotte Street; back in Washington, he vaguely promised federal aid.

Three years later, his Republican challenger stood on the same South Bronx block and said, "Look what big government has done—absolutely nothing has changed."

The system operator was talking, by hotline, to the operator of the New York State power pool, who knew that Con Edison was in trouble.

"You better shed some load," the power pool operator said at 8:56, the time of the second lightning strike. "Because I can't pick up anything from the north, see?"

"Yeah," said the Con Edison controller.

"You better shed load. Shed load, you better shed load. You will lose everything."

"I'm trying. I'm trying."

People confessed to their psychiatrists.

People confessed to priests.

Burglars broke into stores; they broke into Jack's, a Fulton Street army navy store, every few weeks.

Police advised Jack to get a big dog.

"A dog?" he asked. "Tell about the dogs to the fifteen-to-seventeen-year-old kids who need ready cash and got no jobs. They're not afraid of dogs." Not on your life.

Instead, he carpeted his roof with two-by-twelves studded with eight-inch spikes.

"I hate to bother you," the power pool operator said three minutes later, "but you better shed about four hundred megawatts, or you are going to lose everything down there."

"I'm trying."

"You're trying? All you have to do is hit the button to shed it, and then we'll worry about it afterwards. But you got to do something, or they're going to open that Linden, New Jersey, tie on you."

"Yeah, right. Yeah, fine."

Kids traded baseball cards. Sparky Lyle's was hot, and Reggie Jackson's hotter.

Investors, some with inside information, traded stocks.

Poor people traded food stamps for cash, getting 50 cents to the dollar.

The state compared the disposition of blackout cases to similar ones between January and June and found the blackout courts were harsher.

Doctors billed Medicaid for the treatment of patients they hadn't seen in years.

The Yankees won a hundred games, then beat the Royals in the play-offs and the Dodgers in a six-game series.

Con Edison's system operator and the power pool operator were talking, but as Con Edison's president later put it, they weren't communicating.

The system operator kept asking for "help"—more power—from the power pool, not understanding when the power pool operator tried to explain that he could not help because the only feeder from the north still in service was overloaded.

The power pool operator kept urging the system operator to increase local generation, with special attention to the gas turbines that were not yet online.

And the system operator tried.

But a boiler-tube rupture took out East River 5.

A hot-well-pump failure took out two generators at Ravenswood, Queens.

A bad condenser vacuum took out Arthur Kill 3, and a bad feed pump took out Astoria 1.

As for the gas turbines, the system operator had ordered several into service. But he'd sent the operators of several others home earlier in the evening, a routine cost-cutting measure.

Merchants reopened looted stores; merchants who hadn't been looted closed.

The Brownsville decorator made plans to move his shop to the playroom and basement of his Malverne home. Reluctantly: His father had opened the shop in 1918. Without a presser and a sewing-machine operator in Malverne, he would have to do the work of three.

But his wife and his son pleaded, and in the end he concluded that they were probably right. Without the commute and constant worry about the neighborhood, he'd add years to his life.

People begged, and people gave in to people begging.

People begged, and people passed them by.

At 9:08, Con Edison's chief system operator, who was still at home, joined the conversation by phone. The system operator described the emergency as he understood it; the chief rightly concluded that there was trouble between Sprain Brook and Buchanan and perhaps also between Buchanan and its ties to the west. He ordered the system operator to reduce the voltage by 5 percent at all area substations, and to try to get more help from New Jersey and Long Island.

Ten minutes later, the chief ordered the system operator to reduce voltage further. But the power he'd saved was lost, and then some, when an overheated cable running between Pleasant Valley and Leeds expanded and sagged. The sagging cable hit an untrimmed tree, causing a fault that tripped breakers at both ends of the line. Breakers closed as they were supposed to, but the cable was still touching the tree. The breakers opened again and locked, opening up the lines between Leeds and Pleasant Valley and Pleasant Valley and Millwood. The electricity that ran through those lines began to flow through the transformer linking Pleasant Valley to Niagara Mohawk, Central Hudson, and New York State Electric & Gas.

To prevent damage, that transformer tripped automatically.

Con Edison had lost its last 345-kilovolt line to the north.

Voters voted, electing the Democrat who talked the toughest about crime and the budget.

Editors wished the mayor-elect well but predicted that without money, he would have a hard time halting the city's decline.

People painted, crocheted, and wrote.

Two people stared at the space where their car had been parked, wondering if it had been stolen or towed.

"What now?" Con Edison's system operator asked the power pool operator when he called at 9:20.

"You've got to shed load immediately, or you're going to go right down the pipe with everything. You've lost that eighty line there now."

"Lost the eighty line?"

"Yeah. You better shed load immediately."

"Oh."

"At least six hundred megawatts, anyway."

"Yep. OK."

Two minutes passed.

"Will you shed load down there immediately."

LILCO's system operator had just informed the power pool operator he had no choice but to open its Con Edison tie.

"Yeah," the Con Edison system operator said.

"At least a thousand megawatts, or you're going to go right down the pipe."

"All right, pal," the power dispatcher said.

Four more minutes passed.

"I'm going to tell you one more time," the power pool operator said. "If you don't shed about six hundred megawatts of load immediately—"

"He's doing it as fast as he can," the dispatcher said.

A blind saxophonist played "Bright Moments" in a small club filled with smoke.

Runaways sang sad songs on Village sidewalks.

Budding comedians told jokes.

La Bohème was at the New York State Opera; a Handel harp concerto was at Avery Fisher Hall.

A mile down Broadway, people watched people take off all their clothes.

"All you got to do is push a button to get rid of it," the power pool operator said.

"That's what he is doing right now," the dispatcher said.

Actually, it was not one button. It was a coordinated combination of buttons and switches designed to prevent accidental load shedding, each combination controlling a particular area's power.

The system operator had never shed load before; nor had he practiced on a simulator.

"All you got to do is push a button," the power pool operator said.

The system operator had been flicking switches and pressing buttons for four minutes. But he hadn't shed any load, and he knew it. He didn't know how to do it.

Observers who agreed about nothing agreed that the city's future looked bleak.

The last week of each month, people packed up to leave.

Fed up with the noise, the air that you could see, the attitude, the cost, the grime, they couldn't get out soon enough.

But the day after they left, others arrived, wide-eyed and giddy: at long last, living in New York City.

"Shed six hundred megawatts immediately, or you'll lose that Linden line, and you're out of business," the power pool operator said at 9:28. "That's the only thing you have left."

A minute later, an overloaded transformer at Staten Island's Goethals substation failed. Protective relays operating breakers on both sides of the tie between Staten Island and New Jersey tripped the line, and Con Edison was on its own.

The operator was still trying to shed load manually when the automatic load-shedding devices finally kicked in. But by then it was too late. The system was too close to collapse. Automatic load shedding created sudden surpluses and then deficits that the last remaining feeders, voltage regulators, transformers, and local generators couldn't handle.

At 9:36, operators of a few of those local generators, determined to protect equipment from permanent damage, shut them down; others were shut down by their own protective devices.

People fought.
People made up.
People made pasta.
People made love.
People were born, people died.
People laughed, and people cried.

53

Afterward, everyone wanted to know why.

There had to be a reason. People wanted to know what it was.

The city conducted an inquiry into the causes of the blackout. The state conducted one. The federal government conducted two. There were also public and private inquiries into the "preparedness" and "response" of the criminal justice system. There were simple surveys of "commercial damage." And there were sophisticated studies of the blackout's long-term social impact and economic cost. The former chief engineer prepared a brief analysis on the eve of the city's public hearings. Con Edison produced a five-volume final report.

There were no government inquiries into the causes of the looting, and there might have been no comprehensive inquiry at all if Ford Foundation executives hadn't funded one. Frustrated by all the "instant analysis," they commissioned a journalist and a political scientist, who wrote a trenchant 240-page book. The authors examined who looted, when they looted, what they looted, where they looted, and why. They didn't rule out cultural, psychological, and moral factors, particularly the growing belief among the poor that the rich and powerful were horrible hypocrites, expecting the poor to live by codes, rules, and laws that they themselves ignored. But, the authors concluded, the root causes were unemployment, inflation, and poverty, "both in old ghettos and in neighborhoods more recently inhabited by the city's poor."

Many of the people who studied the causes of the blackout also talked of a root cause, especially a "complex managerial failure" at Con Edison. Con Edison executives preferred to talk about immediate causes: lightning, faulty breakers and phase-angle regulators, untrimmed trees, and human error. They planned to expand the Control Center computer system, upgrade the automatic load-shedding equipment, train operators on a simulator, and trim trees. If there was a root cause of the blackout, executives and energy-industry spokespeople said, it was the climate the utility operated in; a climate in which legislators, regulators, and environmentalists had blocked or slowed the utility's efforts to deliver reliable, affordable, and safe power.

The story of the blackout in the black community, wrote the editors of the *Amsterdam News*, was of a bitter division between those who "described" the looters as "animals" or "scum of the earth" and those who described them as the "victims of joblessness and oppression." The only thing misleading about that observation was the phrase "in the black community." The white community was bitterly divided, too.

Con Edison's recommendations for fundamental reform were implicit in its identification of a root cause. Executives called for the repeal of the tax on fossil fuels burned in the city; the relaxation of the prohibition on burning dirty oil and high-sulfur coal in the city; and the speedy approval of the utility's long-stalled plans to build new power plants, power lines, and power storage facilities in and around the city.

"Bitterly divided" didn't mean "evenly divided."
Pollsters asked a group of New Yorkers, more than half of whom were Democrats, why looters looted, offering them the opportunity to say yes or no to each of six possible explanations.

Sixty percent agreed that people looted because "they are the kind . . . who always steal if they think they can get away with it." Large majorities rejected four other explanations: heat, frustration, conflict with store owners, and unemployment. They rejected the sixth—poverty—most overwhelmingly.

Energy regulators, independent investigators, and energy-minded newspaper editors dismissed Con Edison's analysis of the root cause of the blackout as "opportunistic" and its recommendations for reform as merely a "wish list." Both the explanation and the recommendations were ultimately misleading in that they suggested, against all the evidence—including Con Edison's own calculations—that the blackout was caused by a shortage of generating and transmission capability.

Every explanation of the looting, like every explanation of the blackout, contained a prescription: If looters are hungry, you feed them. If they are unemployed, you give them jobs. If they are desperate, you give them hope. Criminals, on the other hand, you jail. Roaches you poison. Animals you cage or shoot.

On the evening of July 13, Con Edison had twice the generating capacity it needed.

The real problem, public and private analysts concluded, was that the utility's generators, transmission network, and protective devices were poorly designed and maintained.

Its operating procedures were penny-wise and pound-foolish.

Its operators were completely unprepared for an emergency.

Its ties to neighboring utilities were fragile at best.

Its communications with customers (who could have reduced power in the hour between lightning flash and outage) were wholly inadequate.

And its emergency backup system and blackout restoration plan were fundamentally flawed.

The argument went on.

The sides were not evenly matched, not even in New York.

But it played well on the talk shows.

Hosts asked:

Poor people or piranha?

Black or white?

Jobs or jails?

Darkness or light?

The Brownsville looter wasn't among the guests on the talk shows, but he got it right: "It's really heavy to get into when you think about why people do certain things.

"But human beings, boy. I'm telling you."

"Regulators and environmentalists had nothing to do with the blackout," said one electrical engineer. "The necessary energy was there, the capability to maintain and deliver it was not."

People continued to talk about the blackout, and the looting.

They talked about why "they" did what they did.

Why they do what they do.

But few managed to "get into it," not the heavy stuff.

No need.

They thought they knew.

Afterword

That July, they thought they knew why. And when the power failed twenty-six years later, in August 2003, they thought they knew again.

Not why the power failed.

No one knew that, and once people were assured that the blackout was just a blackout—not sabotage or a bomb—few people really cared. Initial reports that lightning had caused it (just like 1977, newspeople said) were quickly discredited. The politicians who scrambled to the nearest microphone to blame regulation or deregulation, oilmen or tree huggers, Democrats or Republicans, were by and large ignored. Instant analysis gave way to investigative reporting, and for weeks each day's papers carried the latest theory: overgrown trees; equipment failure; human error; communications mishmash; clueless system operators; computer crashes; the absence of uniform operating standards and procedures; balkanized oversight; unenforced regulations; federal rules violations; utility mismanagement; the structure of the industry; the politics of energy policy; or all of the above: the superpower's third-world power grid.

Officials in Washington, Ottawa, and eight state capitals ordered investigations. Utilities pointed fingers at one another. Experts argued. But the people who knew the most said the least, realizing that it would be months before investigators could collect, organize, and interpret the data—tens of thousands of bits and pieces of information—that might allow them to trace, millisecond by millisecond, the cascade of events that transformed the routine failure of a few power lines into a history-making electrical disaster.

New Yorkers didn't know why the power failed.

What they knew was why, when it did, no one had looted.

They were sure they knew, and it felt really good to say.

The city had changed.

Back in the 1970s, New York had been in desperate straits, wracked by stagflation, strikes, arson, drugs, graffiti, cynicism, a serial killer, stinking subways, white flight, gas lines, high crime, fiscal crisis, and racial strife.

Now it was a different place.

Despite the recession and the fallout from the attack on the World Trade Center, the city's economy was fundamentally sound. The population had topped eight million in 2000, and it continued to grow. New immigrants had revitalized several struggling neighborhoods; artists had revitalized others. A record number of construction workers had built a record number of new homes, and with aid from the city, they had built some of those homes for first-time homeowners in the South Bronx, Harlem, even Bushwick.

It was a new city, pundits said, a city remade. Families were more stable. Streets were cleaner. In the parks, flowers bloomed. The police were tougher. Drug use was on the wane. New Yorkers cared for one another and for New York. Respect for the law had grown. Violent crime was at an all-time low. Selfishness and detachment were out; cooperation, responsibility, and compassion were in vogue. The subways were safe, and often on time. And thanks to Osama Bin Laden and Saddam Hussein, black and white New Yorkers were finally on the same side of the color line.

Some stressed the new civility.

Some stressed the half-life of a long economic boom.

Some stressed the years of tough policing, and its dark side, fear.

Everyone mentioned the difference that the time of day might have made: The power failed at 4:30 in the afternoon, giving the police three and a half hours to mobilize before sunset, and another half hour before dark.

The list of reasons was long, but next to no one argued about which reason was right. People don't get as worked up when bad things don't happen as when they do. In 1977, people had refused to acknowledge that there might be more than one reason why people looted. In 2003, people readily acknowledged that there might be more than one reason why they did not. But, in a way, they were not acknowledging much. Almost all the small reasons added up to one big reason, the reason that felt so good to say:

New York, and New Yorkers, had changed.

What a difference a day had made.

On August 13, and for months before that, most of the talk and writing about the city had been grim: the fitful recovery from recession; the billion-dollar budget deficit; the corporate relocations; the decline in tourism; the narrowly averted transit strike; the layoff of thousands of city workers; the hike in taxes, transit fares, and fees; the closing of firehouses, subway token booths, branch libraries, and outer-borough zoos. Violent crime remained low, but two years after September 11, most New Yorkers expected another terrorist attack, and many said they had simply learned to live with anxiety and fear.

In fact, until the afternoon of August 14, hardly a day had passed without a commentator asking, "Are we living through the 1970s all over again?"

Then the power failed.

There was some panic, and some price gouging. After the sun went down, there were scattered incidents of looting. But the vast majority of people rose to the occasion. Even Con Edison came through. The utility had done "as good a job as could be hoped for," the mayor said.

Things were not so bad after all. Certainly nothing like the 1970s. On the contrary, things were good. And New Yorkers were good too.

That was a comforting comparison, and it lay at the heart of a comforting explanation. But it ignored at least one inconvenient fact: When the power failed in July 1977, most people did pretty much the same things they had done when the power failed in November 1965, and would do again when the power failed in August 2003. Some of them did the exact same things: They evacuated subway trains; hung out on stoops; directed traffic; hosted blackout parties; bagged patients on respirators; walked for miles and miles; carried water to the elderly and infirm; cooked and ate food they feared would spoil.

In 1977, unlike 1965 and 2003, many people looted, and afterward people argued about why. But the vast majority of people—most everyone—in every neighborhood in the city rose to the occasion. They comported themselves admirably, and made their mayor proud.

It was no easier to know for sure why people did not loot in 2003 than it was to know why they did in 1977. It was even harder to explain the reasons with confidence on the news the very evening of the blackout or in the newspapers the next day. Everyone who has ever been asked to analyze an event while it was still happening, or to explain the historical significance of the day's top story, will sympathize with and give credit to all those who tried. The mayor was one who tried: "New Yorkers," he said, "showed that the city that burned in the seventies . . . is now a very different place."

And the mayor was right. The differences are real. The looting was horrible. The city was burning. There is no denying that things have changed. But we should be wary of the pundits' tale of two cities—the sick city and the healthy city, the lean years and the fat years, the bad New Yorkers and the good. Or any other story that suggests that everything or everyone is either one thing or another, that everything or everyone has changed, or remained the same.

New York was a cold place in July 1977, and a caring place. Among those who cared were the people who argued about the looting. Sure, some were opportunists and ideologues seeking to score political points. But many others, on both sides of the argument, cared deeply about the welfare of the city. Many also cared deeply about the welfare of the looters.

New York was a dangerous place in 1977, and it was a safe place. It was a kind place and a cruel place. It was a thrilling place and a frightening place. It could be dark in broad daylight, and bright in the dark. Many people were miserable, and many people were having the time of their lives.

It is all that now. And perhaps what is most thrilling and most frightening is how, in a fraction of a second, for particular people in particular places at particular points in time, it can change from one to the other.

Just ask the people who, on the afternoon of August 14, 2003, were stuck, without a clue, in an elevator in the Empire State Building. One of them was rescued by a detective who rappelled down the shaft, put a harness around him, and hauled him up five floors to safety. Ask the people whose blackout celebrations were spoiled by their careless use of candles. In Greenpoint, two of them were pulled out of the flames by firemen moments before they would have died. Ask all the people who, in that first uncertain hour after the power failed, were suddenly separated from a parent, spouse, or child in the impatient mass of people converging on the Thirty-eighth Street ferry terminal or crossing an East River bridge.

Or ask anyone who has simply been smiled upon by a stranger on a city sidewalk when a smile was the only thing in the city that would do.

Or anyone who saw or heard those hijacked planes in their final seconds of flight and remembers—everyone remembers—the brilliance of the sky over the city that morning: a blinding blue.

Contradictions. Absolutely. A city is large, and it contains multitudes. When we think about it, when we talk about it, when we write about it, when we argue about it—when we try to figure out why our friends and neighbors, let alone total strangers, do the things that they do—we owe it to the city, and to ourselves, to be true to those contradictions. They are our contradictions too.

Notes

The following abbreviations for newspaper titles are used in the Notes:

AN   *Amsterdam News*
NYDN   New York *Daily News*
NYN   *New York Newsday*
NYP   *New York Post*
NYT   *The New York Times*
VV   *The Village Voice*
WP   *The Washington Post*

Chapter 1

4 *There was lightning:* Steve Semken, letter to author, 6 Apr. 1999.
4 *Half the city's power:* Alexander Lurkis, *The Power Brink: Con Edison—A Centennial of Electricity* (New York, 1982); Gerald L. Wilson and Peter Zarakas, "Anatomy of a Blackout: How's and Why's of the Series of Events that Led to the Shutdown of New York's Power in July 1977," *IEEE Spectrum* 15 (Feb. 1978): 38–46.
5 *It is not anyone's idea of a perfect system:* Ibid.

Chapter 2

7 *There were a few signs:* Lurkis, *Power Brink*.
8 *The electrical engineer:* Ibid., 1–2.
9 *When the lights went out in November 1965:* Ibid., 56–61.
9 *The 1965 blackout: Business Week*, 20 Nov. 1965; 6 Nov. 1966; *Newsweek*, 20 Dec. 1965; *Life*, Nov. 1965; Lurkis, *Power Brink*, 56–61.
10 *A relay in Canada:* Ibid.
10 *People stepped off trains: NYN*, 21 July 1977.

11 *Two dozen people:* NYT, 13 July 1977; ABC, CBS, and NBC Evening News, 13 July 1977.

11 *At around nine-thirty:* NYT, 14 July 1977; NYDN, 15 July 1977.

12 *The subway supervisor:* Ibid.

12 *A few people hid from Son of Sam:* Judie Eisenberg, letter to author, 31 Mar. 1999.

13 *"I could see it coming":* NYDN, 15 July 1977. Cf. NYT, 14, 31 July 1977.

14 *The chairman had come to Con Edison:* Lurkis, *Power Brink*, 114–15; *New York*, 1 Aug. 1977; NYT, 14–15 July 1977; NYDN, NYP, 15 July 1977; *Time, Newsweek*, 25 July 1977.

15 *Despite the chairman's best efforts:* Ibid.

16 *Con Edison's customers:* Ibid.

16 *The chairman walked into his den:* New York, 1 Aug. 1977.

Chapter 3

18 *In sealed buildings:* Newsweek, 25 July 1977. See also NYT, 15 July 1977.

19 *On a low floor of a high-rise:* Anonymous, interview, n.d. (1977); for an abridged transcript of this interview, see Robert Curvin and Bruce Porter, *Blackout Looting!: New York City, July 13, 1977* (New York, 1979): 205–18.

19 *"Where's New York?":* Newsweek, 25 July 1977.

20 *Simon Hench:* Thomas C. Wallace, letters to author, 27 Mar., 8 Apr. 1999.

20 *"There was mass confusion":* Anonymous, interview, n.d. (1977); for an abridged transcript of this interview, see Curvin and Porter, *Blackout Looting!*, 188–205.

21 *Mayor Beame:* NYT, NYDN, NYP, 15 July 1977; *Time, Newsweek*, 25 July 1977.

22 *A Brooklyn couple:* Curvin and Porter, *Blackout Looting!*, 13–16.

22 *"How will I ever identify Mr. .44 now?":* Una Kennedy Provenzano, letter to author, 25 Mar. 1999.

22 *"What did you do?":* Michael Daly and Denis Hamill, "Here Comes the Neighborhood," VV 22 (25 July 1977).

23 *The Cubs's Ray Burris:* NYT, 15 July 1977.

23 *Con Edison's acting vice president for public affairs:* Joyce Hergenhan, interview, 4 June 1999.

Chapter 4

25 *Up in Windows on the World: NYT*, 15 July 1977; Judd Woldin, letter to author, 27 Mar. 1999.

25 *For people looking for cabs:* David Ginzberg, letter to author, 21 Mar. 1999.

26 *An apartment full of people:* Meredith Rich, letters to author, 27 Mar., 15 Apr. 1999.

26 *All three television networks: Newsweek*, 25 July 1977; *NYT*, 15 July 1977.

26 *Stoop hangers: NYT*, 14 July 1977.

26 *"It's a citywide blackout":* Thomas C. Wallace, letters to author, 27 Mar., 8 Apr. 1999; Beatrice Williams-Rude, letter to author, n.d. (Mar. 1999).

27 *A young man in an East Side restaurant:* Anonymous, interview, 13 July 1999.

27 *Two Jersey women:* Lillian Leifer, letters to author, 24 Mar., 17 Apr. 1999.

27 *The young Bronx woman:* Una Kennedy Provenzano, letter to author, 25 Mar. 1999.

28 *Four men:* Curvin and Porter, *Blackout Looting!*, 126–29.

28 *Network television: NYT, NYP, NYDN*, 15 July 1977; *Newsweek, Time*, 25 July 1977.

28 *"There was fear mixed with excitement":* Curvin and Porter, *Blackout Looting!*, 8–10.

29 *In a pub on Seventh Avenue: NYDN*, 15 July 1977; anonymous letter to author, 9 June 1999.

29 *People who stole for a living:* Curvin and Porter, *Blackout Looting!*, 39.

29 *There were dancers who kept dancing: NYT, NYDN, NYP*, 15 July 1977.

29 *Standing by the window:* Curvin and Porter, *Blackout Looting!*, 170–71.

29 *On Utica Avenue:* Ibid., 3; *NYDN*, 15 July 1977.

30 *The men of Ladder Company 26:* Daniel P. Higgins, letter to author, 14 Apr. 1999; Higgins, interview, 17 Apr. 1999.

30 *To the delight of the audience: NYT, NYDN, NYP*, 15 July 1977.

30 *A truck pulled up:* Curvin and Porter, *Blackout Looting!*, 23.

30 *Many writers kept writing:* Maggie Bergara, letter to author, 14 Mar. 1999.

31 *On Fulton Street: AN*, 23 July 1977; Curvin and Porter, *Blackout Looting!*, 154.

31 *On Broadway: NYT*, 14 July 1977; Vince Mahler, letter to author, 2 Apr. 1999.

31 *Three men pulled three cars: NYDN*, 15 July 1977.

31 *On Brooklyn's Broadway:* Curvin and Porter, *Blackout Looting!*, 4, 39.

32 *At Fifth Avenue and Fifty-sixth Street:* Howard Heller, interview, 22 Mar. 1999.

32 *A man in his late teens:* Daly and Hamill, "Here Comes the Neighborhood."

32 *The stage manager of* The Merry Widow: *NYDN*, 15 July 1977.

32 *Ladder Company 26 left:* Higgins, letter to author, 14 Apr. 1999; Higgins, interview, 17 Apr. 1999.

33 *A gang of twelve: NYN*, 15 July 1977.

33 *Reporters rushed out to the streets: Newsweek*, 25 July 1977; *NYP*, *NYDN*, 15 July 1977; *NYN*, 16 July 1977.

33 *"High-class dudes":* Curvin and Porter, *Blackout Looting!*, 8–10.

34 *On the thirtieth floor:* Cheryl D. Sandler, letter to author, 23 Mar. 1999.

34 *At the corner of Third Avenue and 105th Street: NYT*, 3 Sept. 1977.

34 *Across the street from Con Edison's corporate headquarters: NYDN*, 15 July 1977.

35 *Up Amsterdam from the guys with the golf clubs: NYT*, 16 July 1977; Curvin and Porter, *Blackout Looting!*, 127–29.

35 *At the yeshiva:* Shlomo Werdiger, letter to author, 16 Apr. 1999.

35 *On the Queens side of the Fifty-ninth Street Bridge: NYDN*, 14 July 1977.

35 *"All the lights are out, everywhere":* Anonymous, interview, n.d. (1977); for an abridged transcript of this interview, see Curvin and Porter, *Blackout Looting!*, 188–205.

Chapter 5

36 *The argument about the causes of the blackout:* Joyce Hergenhan, interview, 4 June 1999. See also *NYP*, *NYDN*, *NYT*, *WP*, 15 July 1977.

Chapter 6

38 *The Bushwick teenager:* Daly and Hamill, "Here Comes the Neighborhood."

39 *Passengers on the seven subways: NYT*, 14 July 1977.

39 *"Everyone's living out his fantasies": NYP*, 15 July 1977.

39 *"We are all black now": NYP*, 15 July 1977.

39 *"Hey, I want to do that":* Rachel Chodorov, interview, 15 Apr. 1999.

40 *"Somebody's got to do the job": NYDN*, 15 July 1977.

40 *The guys with the golf clubs:* Curvin and Porter, *Blackout Looting!,* 126–29.

40 *The volunteers in the intersections:* John H. Zaugg, letters to author, 9, 31 May 1999.

41 *Police informed the mayor: Newsweek,* 25 July 1977; *NYDN,* 15 July 1977.

41 *The men who opened Capri Furniture: NYT,* 16 July 1977; Curvin and Porter, *Blackout Looting!,* 126–29.

41 *The more experienced of the two New Jersey women:* Lillian Leifer, letters to author, 24 Mar., 17 Apr. 1999.

41 *Although they had never done it in the dark:* David Michaelis, "The Darkest City in the World," unpublished manuscript, n.d. (13 July 1977).

41 *"I'll be back": NYDN,* 15 July 1977.

42 *A few men had broken: NYT,* 3 Sept. 1977.

42 *A woman who lived: NYN,* 21 July 1977; *NYT,* 15 July 1977.

42 *Residents of a Brighton Beach: NYDN, NYP,* 15 July 1977.

42 *The Brooklyn man:* Curvin and Porter, *Blackout Looting!,* 13–16.

42 *Two women and a man:* Pete Axthelm, "A Walk on the Wild Side," *Newsweek,* 25 July 1977.

43 *The cast members of* Oh! Calcutta!*:* Michaelis, "The Darkest City in the World." See also *NYT, NYDN,* 15 July 1977.

44 *A crowd followed a brick: New York,* 8 Aug. 1977.

44 *Residents of a welfare hotel: NYP,* 15 July 1977.

44 *The owner of Morris Toyland: NYT,* 3 Sept. 1977.

45 *The young Brownsville man:* Anonymous, interview, n.d. (1977); for an abridged transcript of this interview, see Curvin and Porter, *Blackout Looting!,* 188–205.

45 *Forty minutes into the blackout: NYT,* 14, 15 July 1977. See also *NYP, NYDN, NYN, WP,* 15 July 1977.

45 *At the Metropolitan Opera House: NYDN,* 15 July 1977.

45 *In the intersections of Rego Park: NYP,* 15 July 1977.

45 *A block away: NYP,* 15 July 1977.

46 *People in need: NYN,* 14 July 1977.

46 *Two hundred people stormed: NYN,* 15 July 1977; Curvin and Porter, *Blackout Looting!,* 23.

46 *In the emergency room at Bellevue: NYDN,* 15 July 1977. See also *NYT, NYP,* 15 July 1977.

47 *The lights went out at the Broadway Theatre: NYT,* 15 July 1977; John Hatfield, letter to author, 10 Apr. 1999.

47 *Thirty minutes after he returned to the Waldorf:* Vernon R. Alden, letter to author, 24 Mar. 1999.

47 *In a grocery store on East Eighty-sixth Street: WP*, 24 July 1977.

48 *On the commercial strip in Jackson Heights: NYDN*, 14 July 1977.

48 *When the power went off at* The New York Times*: NYT*, 15 July 1977.

48 *In Jamaica, Queens: NYN*, 15 July 1977.

48 *"Hey, don't let those two guys out of here":* Robert Buckley, letter to author, n.d. (May 1999).

49 *The sidewalks and streets of the theater district:* Rachel J. Lehr, interview, 23 June 2000.

49 *All over the city:* Anonymous, letter to author, 9 June 1999.

Chapter 7

50 *"Animals": NYT*, 15 July 1977.

50 *"They hate everybody": NYP*, 15 July 1977.

50 *"They're crazy": NYT*, 14 July 1977.

50 *"In the last blackout": NYT*, 15 July 1977.

50 *"The looters": NYT*, 15 July 1977.

Chapter 8

51 *The math was simple:* Curvin and Porter, *Blackout Looting!*, 57–77. See also John Hollister Stein, "The Lightless Night of Looting: Lessons from the 1977 New York City Blackout" (Civil Defense Preparedness Agency, Oct. 1978); New York State Crime Control Planning Board, "Report of the Select Committee on Criminal Justice Emergency Preparedness," 31 Oct. 1977; New York City Office of the Deputy Mayor for Criminal Justice, "Report Concerning the Effects of the Blackout of July 13–14, 1977, on the Criminal Justice System in New York City," n.d. (Sept. 1977).

51 *Most of the stores that were saved:* Curvin and Porter, *Blackout Looting!*, 155.

52 *Unable to keep the peace:* Ibid., 64.

52 *Farther west on Fulton Street:* Ibid., 159.

52 *Police hoped to scare the looters:* Ibid., 129.

53 *On 172nd Street in the Bronx:* Jason Vicente, 21 Oct. 1998, Blackout History Project: New York City, 1965/1977 (27 June 2000), http://blackout. gmu.edu/forum.

53 *Some looters and lookouts: NYP*, 15 July 1977.

53 *On the Grand Concourse:* Curvin and Porter, *Blackout Looting!*, 143–44.

53 *The Brownsville looter:* Anonymous interview, n.d. (1977); for an abridged transcript of this interview, see Curvin and Porter, *Blackout Looting!*, 188–205.

54 *On Manhattan's Third Avenue: NYT*, 19 July 1977.

54 *When police dared to get out of their cars: Time*, 25 July 1977.

54 *Two officers who had just: NYDN*, 17 July 1977.

55 *On Utica Avenue: NYP*, 15 July 1977.

55 *The police commissioner:* Curvin and Porter, *Blackout Looting!*, 69–70.

56 *On Willis Avenue in the South Bronx:* Ibid., 24.

56 *On Second Avenue and 109th Street in Manhattan: NYT*, 15 July 1977.

56 *On Broadway and 146th Street: NYN*, 15 July 1977.

56 *It didn't necessarily take machetes: NYT*, 16 July 1977; Curvin and Porter, *Blackout Looting!*, 43–44.

57 *Emboldened by the sight:* Curvin and Porter, *Blackout Looting!*, 9, 43.

57 *Not every act of resistance was successful: NYDN*, 15 July 1977.

57 *Across the street from the second bicycle store:* Curvin and Porter, *Blackout Looting!*, 15.

58 *The owners of LeMans: New York*, 1 Aug. 1977.

58 *On Broadway in Manhattan's West Nineties: NYT*, 14 July 1977.

58 *On 138th Street in the Bronx: NYT*, 13 Nov. 1977.

58 *On East Ninth Street:* Curvin and Porter, *Blackout Looting!*, 169–70.

59 *The Bushwick man:* Ibid., 15.

59 *By early morning: Time*, 25 July 1977. See also Curvin and Porter, *Blackout Looting!*, 57–77.

60 *The owner of the Radio Clinic:* Alan Rubin, interview, 2 June 1999.

60 *Some of the policemen's calm was resignation:* Curvin and Porter, *Blackout Looting!*, 58.

60 *Looters streamed into Key Food:* Daly and Hamill, "Here Comes the Neighborhood."

60 *On Myrtle Avenue: Time*, 25 July 1977.

60 *Some was politics: NYDN*, 15 July 1977.

61 *Just one supermarket was untouched:* Curvin and Porter, *Blackout Looting!*, 50.

61 *And some of the calm was good common sense:* Ibid., 59.

61 *Two officers stood outside a Utica Avenue A&P: NYDN*, 15 July 1977.

Chapter 9

62 *"It was like a fever struck them"*: *Time*, 25 July 1977.

62 *"The looters swept through here like locusts"*: ABC Evening News, 16 July 1977.

62 *"I've seen looting before"*: Curvin and Porter, *Blackout Looting!*, 41.

62 *"You grab four or five"*: *Time*, 25 July 1977.

62 *"In 1965 we were dealing"*: ABC News Special Report, 14 July 1977.

62 *"It's the night of the animals"*: *WP*, 15 July 1977; *Time*, 25 July 1977.

Chapter 10

63 *"This is the greatest"*: *NYP*, 15 July 1977.

63 *"I want to go home"*: Laquarta Little, letters to author, 22 Mar., 22 June 1999.

63 *The stadium light and sound crew*: *NYT*, 15 July 1977.

64 *A Manhattan psychiatrist*: Augustus F. Kinzel, letter to author, 21 Mar. 1999.

64 *"What's up?"*: *NYP*, 15 July 1977.

64 *An NYU undergraduate*: Logan Fox, interview with author, 18 Apr. 2003.

64 *Up and down the "alphabet" avenues*: Curvin and Porter, *Blackout Looting!*, 169–70.

65 *Faintly at first*: Kinzel, letter to author, 21 Mar. 1999.

65 *"There was a riot in the street"*: Curvin and Porter, *Blackout Looting!*, 128–29.

65 *On Stillwell Avenue*: Bethany Cortale, letter to author, 15 Apr. 1999.

66 *On University Avenue*: Curvin and Porter, *Blackout Looting!*, 10–12.

66 *The bagpiper marched*: Kinzel, letter to author, 21 Mar. 1999.

66 *On the steps of one of the row houses*: Curvin and Porter, *Blackout Looting!*, 159–64.

67 *"Our instruments were our livelihoods"*: Howard Heller, interview, 22 Mar. 1999.

67 *The Harlem teenager*: Anonymous, interview, n.d. (1977); for an abridged transcript of this interview, see Curvin and Porter, *Blackout Looting!*, 205–18.

68 *At midnight the jazz trio*: *NYT*, 15 July 1977; Judd Woldin, letter to author, 27 Mar. 1999.

68 *The Brownsville looter*: Anonymous, interview, n.d. (1977); for an abridged transcript of this interview, see Curvin and Porter, *Blackout Looting!*, 188–205.

68 *People without radios:* Daly and Hamill, "Here Comes the Neighborhood." See also *NYT*, 15 July 1977; *Time*, 25 July 1977; *Newsweek*, 25 July 1977.

69 *Aware that the blackout might be a political opportunity: NYT, NYN, NYP, NYDN, WP,* 15–16 July 1977; *Newsweek, Time,* 25 July 1977; *New York,* 1 Aug. 1977; *VV,* 25 July 1977.

69 *Sometime after one a.m.:* Lillian Leifer, letters to author, 24 Mar., 17 Apr. 1999.

69 Newsday *began printing the* Daily News: *NYDN,* 15 July 1977; *Newsweek, Time,* 25 July 1977.

70 *A Harlem man walked:* Anonymous, interview, 13–15 Apr. 1999.

70 *"I must look pretty good to you":* David M. Clive, letter to author, 24 Mar. 1999.

71 *New York Times reporters: NYT,* 15 July 1977.

71 *At one a.m. word had spread: NYN,* 21 July 1977.

71 *"I'm caught in a* M*A*S*H. *nightmare": NYT, NYP,* 15 July 1977.

72 *At four a.m., an NBC News assistant: NYT,* 15 July 1977; *Newsweek,* 25 July 1977.

72 *"We cried": NYDN,* 15 July 1977; Curvin and Porter, *Blackout Looting!,* 144–45.

72 *The* Times *people piled back into the truck: NYT,* 15 July 1977.

73 *Shortly after five: NYT,* 14–15 July 1977; *NYP, NYDN,* 15 July 1977.

73 *Negotiations between the* News *and its drivers' union: Newsweek,* 25 July 1977. See also *NYP, NYDN,* 15 July 1977; *NYN,* 16 July 1977.

73 *On University Avenue in the Bronx: NYN,* 15 July 1977.

Chapter 11

75 *"They are jackals, that's why": AN,* 23 July 1977.

75 *"Why do they do it?": NYDN,* 15 July 1977.

75 *"When you see a black florist": AN,* 23 July 1977.

75 *"When you are hungry and you haven't worked in a long time": NYT,* 15 July 1977.

76 *"When you're hungry, you're hungry":* Curvin and Porter, *Blackout Looting!,* 170–71.

76 *"They don't have no chance out here": NYT,* 15 July 1977.

76 *"In emergencies": NYN,* 15 July 1977.

76 *"Black teenage unemployment": AN,* 23 July 1977.

76 *"Godlessness": NYN,* 29 July 1977.

77 *"God" gave "poor people their bread":* Daly and Hamill, "Here Comes the Neighborhood."

77 *"I don't think it had much to do with the loot":* Curvin and Porter, *Blackout Looting!*, 168.

Chapter 12

78 *One woman, rising before the sun:* NYDN, 21 July 1977.

78 *A twenty-two-year-old who hadn't been to bed:* Daly and Hamill, "Here Comes the Neighborhood."

78 *The men of Ladder Company 26 watched:* Daniel P. Higgins, letter to author, 14 Apr. 1999; Higgins, interview, 17 Apr. 1999.

79 *With backup power still out at Bellevue:* NYT, 15 July 1977.

80 *In the lobby of the Statler Hilton:* Ibid.

80 *Two men stood outside a Columbus Avenue café:* NYDN, 15 July 1977.

80 *A Far Rockaway man:* NYN, 15 July 1977.

81 *The owner of Gramercy Park Hardware:* NYP, 15 July 1977.

81 *On Watkins Street, near the corner:* Albert Isaacson, letter to author, 11 Apr. 1999.

81 *The owner of a West Side deli:* NYT, 15 July 1977.

Chapter 13

82 *"Being that the lights are out":* Newsweek, 25 July 1977.

82 *"I've got three kids":* Time, 25 July 1977.

82 *"We're poor":* Ibid.

82 *"Prices have gone too high":* Ibid.

82 *"Why us, man?":* New York, 8 Aug. 1977.

83 *"Listen":* NYP, 15 July 1977.

83 *"You take your chance when you get your chance":* Time, 25 July 1977.

83 *"It gets dark here every night":* Ibid.

83 *"Why?":* WP, 15 July 1977.

Chapter 14

84 *On 138th Street in the Bronx:* NYP, NYT, 15 July 1977.

84 *The seventeen-year-old in the Harlem high-rise:* Anonymous, interview, n.d. (1977); for an abridged transcript of this interview, see Curvin and Porter, *Blackout Looting!*, 205–18.

85 My only hope is my security: *NYN*, 15 July 1977. In *WP*, 15 July 1977, the same store was called Simon Furniture.

85 *On Pitkin Avenue: NYT*, 15 July 1977.

86 *On West 110th Street in Manhattan:* Ibid.

86 *Half a mile south: NYDN*, 15 July 1977.

86 *In addition to a few fires:* Ross Klavan, letter to author, 22 Mar. 1999.

87 *On the Grand Concourse:* Thomas J. Kelley, interview, 22 Mar. 1999.

87 *As two jewelers: NYP*, 15 July 1977.

87 *Late morning, the manager: WP*, 15 July 1977. See also *NYN*, 15 July 1977.

Chapter 15

89 *"Man, times are hard": AN*, 23 July 1977.

89 *"Looting is never justified": AN*, 23 July 1977.

89 *"The only way we're going to get it": NYDN*, 15 July 1977.

90 *"My prices are competitive": NYT*, 3 Sept. 1977.

90 *"When it's dark": NYDN*, July 15 1977.

90 *"They looted because":* Curvin and Porter, *Blackout Looting!*, 49. See also *AN*, 23 July 1977.

91 *"It was an opportunity": NYN*, 15 July 1977.

91 *"Jobs?": NYDN*, 21 July 1977.

91 *"I think a lot of it was just mass hysteria":* Curvin and Porter, *Blackout Looting!*, 162–63.

92 *"If you didn't jump in when the lights went off": NYP*, 15 July 1977.

92 *"Attitudes have changed": WP*, 16 July 1977.

92 *"Everyone says they should know better":* Ibid.

93 *"I hope you out-of-town people tell it like it is":* Ibid.

93 *"They saw this as a chance": NYN*, 16 July 1977.

93 *"Outside the precinct house":* Ibid.

93 *"A lot of people saw things": NYP*, 15 July 1977.

94 *In 1965, nothing like this:* New York, 1 Aug. 1977.

94 *"Social spending":* Ibid.

94 *"People have seen Watergate felons": NYN*, 15 July 1977.

94 *A twelve-year-old Brooklyn boy:* Daly and Hamill, "Here Comes the Neighborhood."

95 *"Animals": AN*, 23 July 1977.

95 *"You know we weren't animals up here": NYP*, 15 July 1977.

95 *"If there's an opportunity to commit a burglary": NYP*, 16 July 1977; *NYDN*, 17 July 1977.

96 *With "no goddamn jobs":* ABC News Special Report, 14 July 1977.

96 *"I don't blame the looters":* NYT, 12 Aug. 1977.

96 *"I got it coming to me, man":* NYP, 15 July 1977.

Chapter 16

97 *"This is like a wake":* Burtin J. Sheck, interview, 23 Apr. 1999.

97 *Friends and family of Lavey Yitzhak:* Helene Katz Freedman, letters to author, 12 Apr., 5 July 1999.

98 *There was no ice:* NYT, NYN, 15 July 1977.

99 *A young couple strolling:* Peter J. Dougherty, interview, 19 May 1999.

100 *"I am outraged":* NYDN, 15 July 1977.

Chapter 17

102 *The lights went back on:* Newsweek, Time, 25 July 1977; NYT, NYN, WP, 15–16 July 1977.

Chapter 18

103 *The sun was still high:* NYT, 15 July 1977.

103 *A few blocks north:* Michael E. Katz, letter to author, 21 Mar. 1999.

104 *The police commissioner declared:* NYDN, NYT, NYP, 15 July 1977; Daly and Hamill, "Here Comes the Neighborhood."

104 *"It's a motherfucker":* Daly and Hamill, "Here Comes the Neighborhood."

104 *Most stores were closed:* Anonymous, interview, n.d. (1977); for an abridged transcript of this interview, see Curvin and Porter, *Blackout Looting!*, 188–205.

105 *In and around the Brooklyn Criminal Courthouse:* Daly and Hamill, "Here Comes the Neighborhood"; Newsweek, 1 Aug. 1977.

105 *The Brownsville decorator:* Albert Isaacson, letter to author, 11 Apr. 1999.

106 *"The air is fresh":* NYN, 16 July 1977.

Chapter 19

107 *After brief statements:* NYDN, NYN, NYT, WP, 15–16 July 1977; Newsweek, 25 July 1977.

Chapter 20

109 *On Broadway in Bushwick:* Daly and Hamill, "Here Comes the Neighborhood"; anonymous, letter to author, 26 May 1999; anonymous, "Jour-nal," 4, 16 July 1977.

109 *The corrections commissioner:* Daly and Hamill, "Here Comes the Neighborhood."

110 *"I had to learn":* Curvin and Porter, *Blackout Looting!*, 51–53.

110 *Looters would be punished: NYDN*, 15 July 1977.

111 *Shortly before six, a crowd: NYT*, 15 July 1977; Daly and Hamill, "Here Comes the Neighborhood."

111 *By early Thursday evening: NYN*, 15 July 1977.

112 *Brooklyn was the last stop: NYT, NYN, NYP, NYDN, WP*, 15 July 1977; *Newsweek, Time*, 25 July 1977.

Chapter 21

113 *The argument in the streets: NYT*, 15 July 1977.

Chapter 22

114 *Friday morning: NYT, NYN*, 16 July 1977.

114 *"I'm responsible for twenty-five families": NYT*, 16 July 1977; *Time*, 25 July 1977.

115 *Loans: NYT, WP*, 16 July 1977.

115 *Forget about it?: NYT*, 16 July 1977; *Time*, 25 July 1977.

115 *The chairman of the three-year-old:* Curvin and Porter, *Blackout Looting!*, 50–51; *Time*, 25 July 1977.

116 *Nearly four thousand people: NYP, NYT*, 15–16 July 1977.

116 *The president of the Macon Street Block Association: NYN*, 16 July 1977.

116 *The owner of Simon Smalls: AN*, 23 July 1977.

117 *"Close?": NYT, NYDN*, 16 July 1977.

117 *It was the rush of customers: NYN*, 16 July 1977.

117 *They took raw lumber: NYT*, 16 July 1977.

118 *On 138th Street: NYN*, 16 July 1977.

Chapter 23

119 *A* Daily News *columnist:* Jimmy Breslin, "Open Wounds Fester in Heat, Dirt & Smell," *NYDN*, 17 July 1977. See also Daly and Hamill, "Here Comes the Neighborhood."

Chapter 24

122 *Out on the street:* Curvin and Porter, *Blackout Looting!*, 132–38; *NYT*, 24 Oct. 1977; *NYDN*, 1–5 Aug. 1977.

122 *On Broadway a grocer:* Daly and Hamill, "Here Comes the Neighborhood."

123 *"I'm almost 70 years old":* *NYT*, 16 July 1977.

123 *"I am no bleeding heart":* *NYT, NYP, NYDN, NYN, WP*, 15–16 July 1977.

124 *The owner of Al-Bert's:* Daly and Hamill, "Here Comes the Neighborhood."

124 *The National Shoe Store was open:* Ibid.

124 *The mayor returned to Brooklyn:* *NYT*, 16 July 1977.

Chapter 25

126 *The following day, three teenagers:* Nathaniel Sheppard, Jr., "Looters Offer a Passer-By Booty and a Bill of Goods," *NYT*, 17 July 1977.

Chapter 26

129 *Everywhere he went:* *NYT*, 16 July 1977; *WP*, 17 July 1977. Thirty-two policemen were injured in 1968.

129 *"We fought for years":* *NYT*, 17 July 1977.

130 *"Is this a riot?":* Ibid.

131 *Back at City Hall:* Ibid. See also *WP*, 17 July 1977.

Chapter 27

132 *"You still try to justify their behavior":* Hendrik M. Ruitenbeek, letter to editor, 16 July 1977, *NYT*, 23 July 1977.

132 *"I am shocked":* Ronald H. Dropkin, letter to editor, 15 July 1977, *NYT*, 23 July 1977.

133 *Hundreds of people wrote letters:* *NYT*, 17 July 1977. See also *New Yorker*, 8 Aug. 1977.

133 *"Excuses":* William Safire, "Christmas in July," *NYT*, 18 July 1977.

134 *The prominence of a few members: NYT*, 15, 17 July 1977.

134 *"If only we had heeded the lessons of the 1960s":* Edward Cherney, letter to editor, 18 July 1977, *NYT*, 23 July 1977.

135 *"Of course society must protect itself": NYT*, 17 July 1977.

135 *"Rage?":* Tom Shuford, letter to editor, 18 July 1977, *NYT*, 28 July 1977.

135 *Sure there was glee:* Clayton Riley, *"Time Is No Longer Running Out, It's Gone," NYT*, 17 July 1977. See also Riley, "Desperation: The Bitter Fruit of Neglect," *NYN*, 17 July 1977.

136 *"Bah!":* Norman Nash, letter to editor, 16 July 1977, *NYT*, 23 July 1977.

Chapter 28

137 *The criminal courts: NYDN, NYT, NYP, NYDN*, 17–18 July 1977; *VV*, 25 July, 15 Aug. 1977.

137 *Court officials blamed the police: NYT, NYDN, NYP, NYN*, 16–18 July 1977; *VV*, 25 July, 15 Aug. 1977.

138 *Lawyers for the ACLU: NYN*, 18 July 1977; *NYT*, 16–17 July 1977. See also *VV*, 25 July, 15 Aug. 1977.

138 *Prosecutors blamed Legal Aid attorneys: NYT*, 17–18 July 1977; *NYN*, 18 July 1977; *Newsweek*, 1 Aug. 1977; *NYP*, 26 July 1977. See also *VV*, 25 July, 15 Aug. 1977.

Chapter 29

140 *On Sunday, three days after the blackout: NYT*, 18 July 1977.

Chapter 30

142 *First thing Monday morning: NYT*, 19 July 1977.

142 *The Small Business Administration: NYT, NYDN, NYP*, 19 July 1977.

142 *Firemen in Bushwick: NYDN, NYP*, 19 July 1977.

143 *Heat and lightning: NYT*, 19 July 1977.

143 *The lines outside the SBA offices: NYP*, 18 July 1977; *NYT, NYP, NYDN*, 19 July 1977.

143 *It was a ten-alarm blaze:* Ibid.

143 *The mayor remained hopeful:* Ibid.

144 *"Now they know how it feels to be poor":* Ibid.

144 *The president said nothing: NYDN, NYT*, 19 July 1977.

Chapter 31

145 *On Tuesday, Con Edison's chairman: NYT,* 20, 21 July 1977.

Chapter 32

146 *Lawyers for the Emergency Committee: NYN, NYP, NYT, NYDN,* 20–21 July 1977. For the criminal justice system more generally, see also *NYN, NYP, NYT, NYDN,* 15–19 July 1977; *Time, Newsweek,* 25 July 1977; *VV,* 25 July, 1, 8, 15 Aug. 1977; and the notes to Chapter 53 below.

146 *"We are sick and tired": NYT,* 25 July 1977.

Chapter 33

148 *With the mercury above 100: NYT,* 18, 20–21 July 1977.

Chapter 34

149 *The Emergency Committee had asked: NYP,* 20–21 July 1977; *NYN,* 18 July 1977. See also *NYT,* 20–21 July 1977.

149 *Five of the prisoners awaiting arraignment: NYT,* 21 July 1977; *NYP,* 21 July 1977. See also *NYN,* 22 July 1977.

Chapter 35

151 *"Sin began with Adam":* Andrew Young, quoted in *AN,* 23 July 1977.

151 *Does the ambassador:* Patrick Buchanan, "Hungry Folks Rob Food, Andy, Right," *NYDN,* 21 July 1977, and Buchanan, "The Looting: A Night of People Failure," *NYDN,* 19 July 1977.

152 *Unemployment, the president: NYT, NYDN,* 22 July 1977; *NYDN,* 26 July 1977.

153 *The editors of* The New Republic: Unsigned Editorial, "The Mugging of New York," *The New Republic,* 30 July 1977.

153 *The author of a "Talk of the Town" piece: The New Yorker,* 8 Aug. 1977.

Chapter 36

155 *The chairman of the Board of Correction: NYP,* 26 July 1977; *NYDN,* 27–29 July 1977; *NYT,* 27 July 1977.

155 *The most spectacular witness:* Ibid.

155 *The deputy mayor for criminal justice:* Ibid.

156 *The mayor did not attend: NYDN*, 28 July 1977.

Chapter 37

157 *A labor historian:* Herbert G. Gutman, "As for the '02 Kosher-Food Rioters," *NYT*, 21 July, 3 Aug. 1977.

Chapter 38

161 *"Under any reasonable definition": NYT*, 23–24 July 1977. See also *NYP, WP, NYDN*, 23–24 July 1977.

161 *The White House was still considering: NYP*, 23 July 1977; *NYT, NYN, NYDN, WP*, 24 July 1977.

161 *Standing behind the mayor: NYP*, 23 July 1977; *NYT, WP*, 24 July 1977; *NYDN*, 24 July 1977.

162 *"Carter said": NYDN*, 25 July 1977.

Chapter 39

163 *Con Edison had promised: NYT*, 26 July 1977.

Chapter 40

164 *Whether because they couldn't afford it: Time*, 1 Aug. 1977; *NYN*, 23 July 1977.

164 *In an interview on Friday: NYT*, 29–31 July 1977; *NYDN*, 29 July 1977.

165 *The owner of Merchants:* Burtin J. Sheck, interview, 23 Apr. 1999.

166 *Skeptics had mocked: NYDN, NYT*, 27, 29 July 1977.

166 *The owner of a two-story building: NYT*, 27 July 1977.

167 *There was money around: NYT*, 29 July, 6 Aug. 1977. See also *NYDN*, 31 July 1977; *NYP*, 5–6 Aug. 1977.

168 *The owner of Capri Furniture: NYDN*, 21 July 1977.

Chapter 41

169 *"History teaches us":* Diane Ravitch, "Not Always a Matter of Justice," *NYT*, 27 July 1977.

170 *Readers preferred: NYT*, 28 July 1977.

170 *Absolutely not:* Dorothy Binn, letter to editor, 29 July 1977; *NYT*, 6 Aug. 1977.

Chapter 42

172 *Even the mayor's opponents:* See, for example, *WP*, 25 July 1977; *NYT*, 31 July, 7 Aug. 1977.

172 *At the end of July: NYT, NYP,* 30 July 1977. See also *NYP*, 4 Aug. 1977.

173 *All six of the Democrats: AN*, 23 July 1977; *NYT*, 21, 30 July 1977. See also *NYDN*, 26–27 July 1977.

173 *"First he lost control of the municipal unions": NYT*, 17, 30 July, 2 Sept. 1977.

174 *In retrospect: New York*, 1 Aug. 1977.

Chapter 43

175 *On a television talk show: NYDN*, 25–26 July 1977.

175 *Public officials continued: NYT*, 4–5 Aug. 1977. See also *NYDN, NYP*, 4–5 Aug. 1977.

176 *Two hours later: NYT*, 5 Aug. 1977.

176 *"We would all perhaps like to think":* Ibid.

Chapter 44

177 *"Soon the rats and the roaches": NYT*, 12 Aug. 1977.

177 *The president of the Urban League: AN*, 23 July 1977; *NYDN, NYT*, 25 July 1977.

177 *The streets of Bushwick: NYT*, 12 Aug., 24 Oct. 1977.

178 *Founded by Peter Stuyvesant:* Kenneth T. Jackson and John B. Manbeck, eds., *The Neighborhoods of Brooklyn* (New Haven, 1998), 44–48; Curvin and Porter, *Blackout Looting!*, 132–38. See also Daly and Hamill, "Here Comes the Neighborhood"; *VV*, 8 Aug. 1977; and *NYDN*, 1–5 Aug. 1977.

179 *The editors of* The New York Times: *NYT*, 19 July 1977. See also *NYT*, 24 July 1977.

179 *What happened next was ugly: NYT*, 12 Aug., 24 Oct. 1977; *NYDN*, 1–5 Aug. 1977. The literature on "urban decline" and the "urban crisis" is vast. Particularly useful for my purposes were Ken Auletta, *The Streets Were Paved with Gold* (New York, 1979); Kenneth T. Jackson, *Crabgrass*

Frontier: The Suburbanization of the United States (New York, 1985); Jonathan Rieder, *Canarsie: The Jews and Italians of Brooklyn Against Liberalism* (Cambridge, Mass., 1985); Hillel Levine and Lawrence Harmon, *The Death of an American Jewish Community: A Tragedy of Good Intentions* (New York, 1992); Jim Sleeper, *The Closest of Strangers: Liberalism and the Politics of Race in New York* (New York, 1990); John T. McGreevy, *Parish Boundaries: The Catholic Encounter with Race in the Twentieth-Century Urban North* (Chicago, 1996); and Thomas J. Sugrue, *The Origins of the Urban Crisis: Race and Inequality in Postwar Detroit* (Princeton, 1996).

180 *New York's junior senator: NYDN*, 27 July 1977.

180 *Bushwick seemed to have hit bottom: NYT*, 12 Aug., 24 Oct. 1977.

181 *The* Daily News's *Washington columnist: NYDN*, 18 July 1977.

181 *Bushwick was a story: NYT*, 12 Aug. 1977.

182 *The president, said the president's press secretary: NYDN*, 27 July 1977.

Chapter 45

183 *"The morals of piranha"*: George F. Will, *NYP, NYN, WP*, et al., 21 July 1977. In *The Washington Post*, the end of Will's essay reads: "many people who lack the economic skills and acquired civility necessary for life in free and lawful society."

184 *Animals, rabble, parasites, and piranha:* Anthony Lewis, "Mind of the North," *NYT*, 15 Aug. 1977.

184 *A prominent social critic:* Midge Decter, "Looting and Liberal Racism," *Commentary* 64 (Sept. 1977).

184 *Whatever the epithet:* Lewis, "Mind of the North."

184 *The social critic thought:* Decter, "Looting and Liberal Racism."

185 *"Moralistic bilge":* Irving Howe, "The 'Animals' & the Moralists," *Dissent* 24 (Fall 1977).

186 *The editors of the* Amsterdam News*: AN*, 23 July 1977.

187 *To understand the looting:* Lewis, "Mind of the North."

187 *It was cant to talk about unemployment:* Decter, "Looting and Liberal Racism."

Chapter 46

189 *On Sunday, August 7:* My account of the rush for the blackout cleanup jobs is based on *NYDN*, 7–10 Aug. 1977; *NYP*, 8–10 Aug. 1977; and *NYT*, 9, 11 Aug. 1977.

Chapter 47

192 *At the end of August: NYT*, 25 Aug. 1977. See also *NYT*, 29 Aug. 1977.

Chapter 48

194 *"Nearly half of Brooklyn's looters": NYP*, 8 Aug. 1977; *NYT*, *NYDN*, 9 Aug. 1977.

194 *The Brooklyn DA said that his "hard facts":* Ibid.

194 *In the rush from press conference:* Curvin and Porter, *Blackout Looting!*, 85–96.

195 *The deputy mayor for criminal justice: NYT*, 14 Aug. 1977.

195 *"The first comprehensive survey":* Ibid.

195 *The deputy mayor had cautioned:* Curvin and Porter, *Blackout Looting!*, 85–96. See also New York City Criminal Justice Agency, "A Demographic Profile of Defendants Arrested in the New York City Blackout: A Preliminary Report Prepared by the New York City Criminal Justice Agency," Aug. 1977; New York State Division of Criminal Justice Services, "Report to the Select Committee on Criminal Justice Preparedness: Defendants Arrested As a Result of the New York City Blackout, July 13 and 14, 1977," 8 Sept. 1977.

Chapter 49

197 *City, state, and federal investigators:* See, for example: *NYT*, 26–29 July, 1, 10, 17 Sept. 1977. See also *NYT*, 29 Dec. 1977, 13 July 1978.

Chapter 50

198 *As the city prepared: NYT*, 16 Aug., 2 Sept. 1977.

198 *Three-quarters citywide: NYT*, 3 Sept. 1977.

199 *Under pressure from city officials:* Burtin J. Sheck, interview, 23 Apr. 1999.

199 *Standing in the shell of his store: NYT*, 13 Nov. 1977.

Chapter 51

201 *"Why did you do it?":* This entire chapter is based on two anonymous in-
terviews, n.d. (1977) and Curvin and Porter, *Blackout Looting!*, 12–16.
For abridged transcripts of those interviews, see Curvin and Porter,
Blackout Looting!, 187–218.

Chapter 52

207 *The lightning had struck:* My re-creation of some of the events that led to
the 1977 blackout is based on Wilson and Zarakas, "Anatomy of a
Blackout: How's and Why's of the Series of Events that Led to the
Shutdown of New York's Power in July 1977," *IEEE Spectrum* 15
(Feb. 1978): 38–46; Jack Feinstein, "Learning from Experiences: Case
Study 1, 1977 Con Edison Blackout," n.d., Blackout History Project:
New York City, 1965/1977 (27 June 2000), http://blackout.gmu.edu/
archive/a_1977.html; Feinstein, "Lessons Learned from the 1977 Black-
out: Case Study 1, Sequence of Events," n.d., Blackout History Project:
New York City, 1965/1977 (27 June 2000), http://blackout.gmu.edu/
archive/a_1977.html; Norman M. Clapp, "A Report by a Staff Task
Force from the Department of Public Service to the Governor of the State
of New York on the Events Leading to the Consolidated Edison Company
Blackout of July 13, 1977," 3 Aug. 1977; Clapp, "New York State Investigation of the New York City Blackout of July 13, 1977," Jan. 1978;
New York City, Special Commission of Inquiry into Energy Failures, "Report of the Special Commission," 2 vols., 1 Dec. 1977; U.S. Congress,
House of Representatives, *Hearing Before the Subcommittee on Energy
and Power of the Committee on Interstate and Foreign Commerce: The
New York City Blackout of July 13, 1977*, 95th Cong., 13 Oct. 1977
(Washington, 1978); U.S. Department of Energy, Federal Energy Regu-
latory Commission, "The Con Edison Power Failure of July 13 and 14,
1977" (Washington, 1978); *NYT*, 13 July–17 Sept. 1977.

209 *Street vendors:* For the WINS flashlights, Ross Klavan, letter to author,
22 Mar. 1999.

210 *People tried to pay inspectors:* Jane L. Corwin and William T. Miles,
"Impact Assessment of the 1977 New York City Blackout Prepared for
Lester H. Fink, Division of Electric Energy Systems, U.S. Department of
Energy" (Palo Alto: Systems Control, Inc., July 1978, typed), Blackout
History Project: New York City, 1965/1977 (27 June 2000), http://
blackout.gmu.edu/archive/a_1977.html; Robert Sugarman, "New York

City's Blackout: A $350 Million Drain," *IEEE Spectrum* 15 (Nov. 1978):
44–46.

212 *People confessed to their psychiatrists:* For Jack's, see Curvin and Porter,
Blackout Looting!, 53.

213 *Kids traded baseball cards:* For the disposition of the blackout cases, see
NYP, 15 Aug. 1977; *NYT*, 16 Aug., 15 Sept. 1977, 13 Jan., 23 Apr., 13 July
1978; and especially Curvin and Porter, *Blackout Looting!*, 97–109.

Chapter 53

218 *The city conducted an inquiry:* See, for example, Stein, "The Lightless
Night of Looting: Lessons from the 1977 New York City Blackout"; New
York State Crime Control Planning Board, "Report of the Select Commit-
tee on Criminal Justice Emergency Preparedness," 31 Oct. 1977; New
York City, Office of the Deputy Mayor for Criminal Justice, "Report Con-
cerning the Effects of the Blackout of July 13–14, 1977, on the Criminal
Justice System in New York City," n.d. (Sept. 1977); Corwin and Miles,
"Impact Assessment of the 1977 New York City Blackout Prepared
for Lester H. Fink"; Robert Sugarman, "New York City's Blackout: A
$350 Million Drain," *IEEE Spectrum* 15 (Nov. 1978): 44–46; and
Lurkis, *Power Brink*, 75–80. See also the public inquiries into the causes
of the power failure cited in the first note to Chapter 52 above.

218 *There were no government inquiries:* See Curvin and Porter, *Blackout
Looting!*. See also Gregory L. Muhlin, Louis E. Genevie, Elmer L. Struen-
ing, Seymour R. Kaplan, and Harris B. Peck, "Comparative Neighbor-
hood Characteristics: An Analysis of the 1977 Blackout Looting in New
York City" (paper presented to the Society for the Studies of Social Prob-
lems, Toronto, Canada, Aug. 1981); Gregory L. Muhlin, Patricia Cohen,
Elmer L. Struening, Louis E. Genevie, Seymour R. Kaplan, and Harris B.
Peck, "Behavioral Epidemiology and Social Area Analysis: The Study of
Blackout Looting," *Evaluation and Program Planning* 4 (1981): 35–42;
Ernest H. Wohlenberg, "The 'Geography of Civility' Revisited: New York
Blackout Looting, 1977," *Economic Geography* 58 (1982): 29–44;
Louis E. Genevie, Seymour Kaplan, Harris Peck, Elmer L. Struening,
June E. Kallos, Gregory L. Muhlin, and Arthur Richardson, "Predictors
of Looting in Selected Neighborhoods of New York City During the
Blackout of 1977," *Sociology and Social Research* 71 (Apr. 1987):
228–31.

219 *Many of the people who studied the causes:* See, for example, *NYT*,

29 Dec. 1977, 13 July 1978; T. J. Nagel, letter to editor, 15 Aug. 1977, *NYT*, 22 Aug. 1977.

219 *The story of the blackout in the black community: AN*, 23 July 1977.

219 *Con Edison's recommendations:* See, for example, *NYT*, 29 Dec. 1977, 13 July 1978.

220 *Energy regulators, independent investigators:* See, for example, *NYT*, 4–5 Aug., 10 Sept.; Charles Komanoff, letter to editor, 24 Aug. 1977, *NYT*, 3 Sept. 1977.

220 *On the evening of July 13:* Komanoff, letter to editor, *NYT*.

221 *"Regulators and environmentalists":* Ibid.

Afterword

225 *There was some panic: NYT*, 16 August 2003.

226 *The mayor was one who tried: NYT*, 16 August 2003.

Acknowledgments

Hundreds of New Yorkers and former New Yorkers wrote to me to share their memories, thoughts, and stories. Although I cannot acknowledge every one of them here, I am grateful to every one of them, including all those who knowingly or unknowingly shared stories of 1965. I am also grateful to the editors of *The New York Review of Books* and *The New York Times Book Review* for again printing my author's query.

For time to write, I would like to thank the John Simon Guggenheim Foundation; Princeton University's Shelby Cullom Davis Center for Historical Studies; and Rutgers University, Newark. Special thanks to Anthony Grafton, Kari Hoover, Kenneth Mills, and their colleagues in the history department at Princeton for their patience and understanding over the course of a difficult year. Steven Diner, Sallie Kasper, and Edward Kirby—all at Rutgers—have been patient and understanding for six years.

Mt agent, Anne Edelstein, my Rutgers colleague Jan Lewis, and my editor, Rebecca Saletan, were this book's first fans, and they have remained faithful to the very end. They somehow knew what I was trying to do, and through more drafts than anyone would believe, they have helped me do it better. At Farrar, Straus and Giroux, I am also grateful to Maggie Carr, Stacia Decker, Cary Goldstein, Debra Helfand, Spenser Lee, Jonathan Lippincott, Don McConnell, Susan Mitchell, John Rambow, Peter Richardson, Jeff Seroy, and Beth Thomas. Would that I could write a good book as swiftly and surely as they can make one.

For all sorts of other things, and just about everything, I would like to thank Maggie Bergara, Barry Bienstock, Rachel Chodorov, Dorcas Cofer, Solomon Cohen, Robert Curvin, John Demos, Bruce Dorsey, Finis Dunaway, Daniel Ernst, Joy Ernst, Jody Falco, Nydia Garcia–Preto, Richard Gaskins, James Grimmelmann, Paul Haran, Joyce Hergenhan, Ellen Herman, Daniel Higgins, Martha Hodes, Laura Kalman, Stanley Katz, Kara Kelly, Linda Kerber, Ross Klavan, Diane Klein, Charles Komanoff, Alexander Lurkis, John McGreevy, James McPherson, Anthony McWhorter, Jani Masur, Louis Masur, David Michaelis, Matthew Moore, N. Polinsky, Bruce Porter, Robin Ridler, Daniel Rodgers, Jonathan Rosenberg, Robert Rosenstone, Alan Rubin, Beryl Satter, Burtin Sheck, James Sparrow, Christine Stansell, Jeffrey Steinman, Emilie Stewart, Judith Vichniac, Sean Wilentz, Jeffrey Fischer, Eliza McFeely, Drake McFeely, Karen McFeely, Mary McFeely, William McFeely, Leonard Tesler, Wendy Goodman, Sandra Goodman, Robert Goodman, Jill Mohrer, Jonathan Mohrer, Elayne Goodman, Burton Goodman, and Rachel Lehr.

Finally, I have dedicated this book to Jackson Goodman, Jennifer McFeely, and Samuel Goodman, three New Yorkers who know and understand that life, good life, goes on in the dark as well as in the light.